From the first page, Rene draws you into the lives of a family in turmoil. Her reflective description of the inadequacies of the family social service system and lack of coordination is disturbingly haunting. A must read!

Marty Tanner

Whose Best Interest? Is a book that chronicles the lives of two special children who have been subjected to the yo-yo effect of the Social Services system in two states and several cities across the United States. Having parents who can't take care of themselves, who fail at their jobs (in spite of being educated), and who choose self- absorption as a way of life forces these children to endure negligence, abuse, and injustice.

This journal records years of detail in an effort to expose the need for change in within the Department of Family Services, and documents the ongoing struggle of these two children. They continue to be returned to their mother who doesn't and can't take care of them. It is an ingrained way of thinking: a mother should be taking care of her children. Sometimes other options are better. What is best for the children is determined by a system of case workers who have been trained that reunification of the family is the road best traveled, to the point of tunnel vision. Read along and witness the heartbreaking and sometimes funny events that determine the lives Joel and Fancy Free. You will be spellbound with the drama. And you will want resolution.

Ava Munoz

From the first chapter of this emotional roller coaster ride, you will be hooked, as I was. What started out as a journal of facts and occurrences detailing how the Division of Family Services works, turned into a truly heartfelt story. Reading each chapter made me eager to continue to the next, with the hope that these children would remain with a loving family. Rene and her family stepped in and did whatever they could to help Fancy Free and Joel survive and flourish, whether it was financial or emotional. It's heartbreaking to see that the best of intentions and what is right for a child is no match for the legal system. How children can be returned, time and time again to parents that cannot, or won't provide even some of the most basis needs or nurturing is heart rendering. You won't be able to put this story down and definitely will not get it out of your mind when finished.

Geri Steckel

Whose Best Interest?

a fight to save two american kids

Rene Howitt

Whose Best Interest?
a fight to save two american kids

TATE PUBLISHING & Enterprises

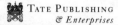 TATE PUBLISHING
& Enterprises

Tate Publishing is committed to excellence in the publishing industry. Our staff of highly trained
professionals, including editors, graphic designers, and marketing personnel, work together to produce
the very finest books available. The company reflects the philosophy established by the founders, based
on Psalms 68:11,

"THE LORD GAVE THE WORD AND GREAT WAS THE COMPANY OF THOSE WHO PUBLISHED IT."

If you would like further information, please contact us:
1.888.361.9473 | www.tatepublishing.com
TATE PUBLISHING & Enterprises, LLC | 127 E. Trade Center Terrace
Mustang, Oklahoma 73064 USA

Published in the United States of America

ISBN: 1–5988682–2–5
06.12.05

Disclaimer

The events that take place in this story are presented from my personal point of view. This is what my heart and eyes experienced. If any other person involved in this account were to put this to paper their version may differ, based on their perspective, history, and personal accountability. All of the names of persons and companies have been changed to protect their identity. All city and county names within the states have also been changed. The movement of the parents within the state of Missouri was limited to a more specific area and therefore no city name is mentioned. However, because the movement of the mother in the state of Alabama encompasses so many different locations I have chosen to name cities that are not the actual locations of where the events took place.

The intent of this book is not to further put into ruin what these adults have already set out to destroy, however to open the eyes of the public as to the short comings of the system I believe we have in place to protect our innocent children. The purpose of this work is to use this story to get the voting public to become upset enough over this issue that politicians know they must change a dysfunctional system. We as a society need to know that our lawmakers and politicians are working towards meaningful and effective changes.

Lucas and I met a year and a half before he graduated from college. Shortly after he earned his degree in finance and got a job as a bank examiner, we married. I was twenty-one and Lucas was twenty-three. We spent four years enjoying life with each other before our first child, Lindsay, came along and Lucas started to advance in his career. Three years later we had our second daughter, Nikki, and four years after that Julia was born. All the while, Lucas's banking career continued to advance. When Nikki was two years old I was able to become a stay-at-home mom. By the time she was five, Lindsay was eight, and Julia was two, Lucas had become the president of a large bank and its holding company. With our humble backgrounds, neither of us had ever dreamed it possible.

The downside? All the time Lucas had to spend working and entertaining with clients and potential customers. Our marriage and our friendship felt the strain of time apart. Meanwhile, our girls were very active in soccer, tennis, softball, and dance.

Lucas and I have both always gone the extra mile to remain physically fit and attractive to each other. Over the years, Lucas took up golf and Indian ball. I took up tennis. Lucas's career along with the children's activities and our own led us to drift apart.

Then a series of events began that were largely out of our control. Events if we could have controlled them, may have turned out very differently. However, God controlled things, not us.

Suddenly the board of directors at Lucas's bank decided, in a five-to-four vote, to sell both the bank and the holding company. Lucas was on the losing side of that vote. He was initially offered a position with the purchasers, but they reneged, and Lucas found himself, at the age of forty-four, unemployed. We weren't hurting for money, as we had owned a large stake in the bank, but the impact of losing his job hit Lucas hard.

The bank transaction closed in September 2001. Lucas and I, for the first time, felt unfocused. He enjoyed his freedom, the money, sleeping in, playing an active role in his daughters' lives, and getting to spend time alone with me during the day. We could actually talk uninterrupted. I valued getting to know my husband again as a friend and not just a provider. Still, we were out of sorts. What was he, what were we, supposed to do with the rest of our lives? Our daughters were by now eighteen, fifteen, and eleven. We were over the hump in terms of the workload of child rearing.

That December, another event took place that changed our lives in ways that we could not imagine.

During the two years prior to the sale of the bank, Lucas and I had witnessed the neglect of two children who were very dear to us: Lucas's nephew, Joel, and Joel's half-sister, Fancy Free. We watched the decline of their parents' relationship and emotional stability. We gave them tremendous financial help and took the children into our home as often as possible to get them away from the madness. In December 2001, it became obvious that the Division of Family Services needed to be made aware of the situation.

Dealing with Family Services and the family court system for more than four years finally prompted me to write this book. Its purpose is not to attack the system our states have in place to provide protection for children such as Joel and Fancy Free, but rather to open the public eye to how the system's shortcomings affect all of us. And to prompt the reader to think about what we can do as communities or as a society to enable the government to change the system.

I'm going to take you along on our journey to fight our way through the system for the sake of Joel and Fancy Free. For a time my husband, Lucas, and I were foster parents to these two beautiful kids, even though Fancy Free is not our blood relative and we knew we had almost no legal chance to keep her.

Keep in mind as you read our story and start to become angry that there are two very legitimate reasons the child welfare system is set up the way it is. First, almost everyone who works within it will tell you that they are restrained financially. Second, this is my own personal observation, there is no place to send the children. What do we do with all of the children in this country who find them-selves in abusive or neglectful homes? Maybe because of the system, it appears there just aren't enough responsible, loving adults willing to take these children in. That's the plain truth.

Let's face it: if there were more loving, open homes than suffering children, no system would have to put up with any nonsense from the biological parents of those children. As it is, abusive parents have the upper hand. If the courts gained the upper hand, then they could address more pressing matters. Like enforcing a "Child in Jeopardy" law. If the Division of Family Services has evidence that a child is being severely abused or neglected, the courts should have the right and the obligation to look at this evidence, even if it violates the rights of the parents. What other chance do young children have, who are not allowed to speak for themselves directly to the judge in court? In fact, the whole mission statement of Family Services needs desperately to be addressed. The statement: to "Reunite the Family" because of this mandate every act and every policy is set up with this one goal in mind. Agencies spend vast amounts of money giving parents one chance after another to screw up and then to reform, only to screw up again. Their mission statement should be: "Protect the Child." Err on the side of the children, at least parents are adults who have some understanding, who can get an attorney to fight for them and be a voice for them. What can a child do but cry?

PART ONE

Chapter One

Our second day in Los Cabos, Mexico was bright and sunny, but my thoughts of Fancy Free and Joel were dark. Lucas and I had traveled there to celebrate our twenty-fifth anniversary. When I called home at sunset to check on Julia, she put down her soda and turned her attention from the TV long enough to tell me that her aunt Maria had called with an update on the kids. It was the first update in more than seven months. Once again, Endora had whisked her children away to places unknown. For the rest of that evening, I thought and prayed. As I went to bed I found myself thinking about how the whole ordeal had started.

1998: Six years earlier. Lucas and I had gone to Branson for a three-day banking conference. I didn't want to go. With three daughters between the ages of eight and fifteen, and Christmas approaching, I had more than enough to do at home. But I told myself that everything would get done and I should enjoy a couple of days away with my husband. We arrived late morning, so Lucas decided to blow off the first day's meetings and spend the day with me.

At 4:00 that afternoon, Lucas's brother Richard called. I gleaned from Lucas's end of the conversation that family trouble was the subject. The "who" and "why" shocked me, but in hindsight I should have seen it coming. Lucas's sister Maria had warned me for years that Richard was trouble.

Lucas hung up the phone. "Sit down. You're not going to believe what I have to tell you." Richard had gotten involved in an extramarital affair, and now the woman was pregnant with his child. So what? Happens all the time. Not much to write a book about.

Lucas had two brothers and four sisters. Richard was the oldest and Lucas the youngest, twelve years apart. They were all born and raised in Missouri. Lucas and the other five siblings grew up very close; in large families, the attention you can't get from mom and dad you get from your siblings. But Lucas didn't get that attention from Richard, who was around very little by the time the youngest came along. Richard also had little patience for Mark and Maria, who were the class clowns. They both goofed off too much.

Richard: that's what people called him until his life fell apart. When this all started, he was a fifty-four year old assistant prosecuting attorney in Huntsville, Alabama. He had been married for twenty-five years to a Croatian woman named Natasha, and had raised three sons from this marriage, Bert, William, and Joseph, ages fourteen to twenty-five. Richard was a retired colonel in the U.S. Air Force. He had served for twenty years as an attorney and an instructor.

He looked like a typical retired military man: hair cut very short and close to his head, slim, posture tall and erect. He had an all-legs kind of physique. Not a handsome man, his nose too big and his heavy glasses constantly sliding down, requiring him to constantly push them back up. Despite his well-groomed military appearance, his gait resembled Walter Matthau's, with long, ambling legs that never looked good in jeans, no matter how expensive.

Richard served in Vietnam and came back a decorated hero. After his tour he married Natasha and enrolled in law school. The Air Force paid for his degree, so he would owe them several more years once he obtained it. We never saw much of Richard, what with Natasha, then their first son, duties on the base, and his law studies. His graduation marked the start of a journey with many stops, wherever the Air Force needed him for a time. After a stint in Germany, he returned to the States and his last stop: Alabama. At the end of that assignment he decided he'd had enough of the military, and retired from the Air Force as a colonel. He planned to return to Missouri and become a public prosecutor. This worked for a while, but not for Natasha, especially when Richard decided to start up with an old flame. My guess is that they wanted to keep the marriage together for Bert, William, and Joseph. So they returned to Alabama, where Richard became an assistant prosecutor. They should have done well financially, thanks to Richard's Air Force pension, along with his new salary.

Richard's job became his life. Passionate about his work, he buried himself in it. He loved pursuing the bad guys and watching them as they received the harshest possible sentence. He bragged about his victories and his unfailing ability to outsmart defense attorneys. His wife, meanwhile, had a lot of time on her hands with all the boys in school. Spending money became a favorite pastime. Richard cared very little for the comings and goings of everyday domestic life, so Natasha handled all of the household decisions, including the boys and the budget.

Richard was a brilliant man by academic standards who fell short in the common sense department. None of us realized this until the story I'm telling began to unfold. He was away from us so much that no one ever had a chance to see him make everyday decisions. Despite the distance, Lucas had always idolized his brother. Richard was the oldest and had achieved great success, and Lucas was the youngest and hoped to do so. It never occurred to Lucas to see the shortcomings in his brother. After being around the family for a while, I concluded that Richard was intelligent but as boring as a chess match. Everyone else in Lucas's family was highly intelligent, but could converse naturally with an average person like me. Try to discuss anything with Richard, from the latest celebrity murder trial to the war in Iraq, and he would talk so far over your head that you'd have to strain your neck to catch the words.

Now, after watching my husband spend five of the last six years helping this man, I see a much more complete picture. Endora was the other woman. She is large and exotic looking, about six feet tall, with ample breasts. I have never seen her thin. She surrounded her dark brown eyes with heavy mascara and eyeliner. High cheekbones protruded from her face. Her dark hair was thin and flyaway. The kind of hair that is very hard to manage. I sometimes thought that if she was thinner and happier she would be a pretty woman. But she wasn't, and her features painted a picture of deep emotional troubles.

Since my knowledge of her is limited to what she and Richard told us, and she is a habitual liar, and Richard met her only a year before we did, the biography I detail here may or may not be true. She was born and raised in Alabama. When she and Richard met, she was a doctor in her late thirties. Since then, her medical license has been revoked twice, that I know of. The first time she was prosecuted and found guilty of Medicare fraud. Guess who the prosecutor was?

Endora's father died when she was eight or nine years old. Her brother is a doctor, and her sister a professor. Her mother suffered from a serious mental illness that she apparently inherited from Endora's grandparents, and endured several shock treatments back in the seventies that left her looking like a zombie. Endora once revealed that one of her grandparents killed the other and then committed suicide. Assuming these stories were true, Endora was at least the third generation in her family to have severe mental problems. She had been diagnosed with adult ADD, bipolar disorder, and manic depression. Endora and Richard claimed that all of her problems stemmed from ADD. My observations told me that ADD was the least of her problems: I met her mother.

After Endora's father died, she and her siblings were passed around among different family members. They would live with their mom until she needed more treatment, and then go off to stay with another aunt or uncle. Social Services may have played a role, but I can't be sure. Somehow Endora put herself through college and medical school. Her other siblings can also boast of impressive academic accomplishments. How could someone suffering from such severe ADD get through medical school without anyone noticing and offering treatment? Good question. But she maintains that it's at the root of her problems. Like Richard, I don't think she was blessed with an abundance of common sense.

Chapter Two

Endora worked with a group of general practitioners whom were being investigated and were ultimately charged with Medicare fraud. The district attorney's office decided to prosecute each doctor separately, rather than go after the group as a whole. Richard was the prosecutor assigned to Endora's case.

Richard lived with his wife of twenty-five years, Natasha, and their three sons. The marriage had been unstable for years, with his extramarital relationships and the financial strain caused by her spending habits almost proving to be too much for them.

Endora was single, sharing a five-thousand-square-foot home with no one but herself. She had hired a contractor to do some remodeling on the house, and was living the kind of life many young people dream of living. She made great money and was treated with the respect that came with a medical degree. At that time, she looked good and stayed fit by working out regularly. She must have played regularly, because by the time she met Richard she told me she had already had three abortions.

Since the wheels of justice turn very slowly in the United States, Endora still had a job working as a doctor in a clinic while she waited her day in court. During that time she embarked on a sexual relationship with the man she had hired to make improvements on her home. She got pregnant again, and decided that it would be a good idea to have the child this time. Why? She was under indictment and faced the strong possibility of losing her license to practice medicine! Then again, unlike the three previous pregnancies, this one might keep her from serving time in jail.

Despite his role as her prosecutor, Endora developed an interest in Richard's personal life. One day, in her attorney's office, she inquired about it. Endora' lawyer told her of Richard's unhappy marriage. Apparently it was no secret. Endora later told me that she decided to pursue a relationship with Richard at that moment. Eventually, despite the glaring conflict and despite his wife, Richard took the bait. He thought Endora was a "knockout," at least compared to Natasha. Not surprisingly, his marriage spiraled downward even further. Their money problems worsened, as he tried in vain to keep up with his financial responsibilities at home while wining and dining his new lady.

Despite their clandestine involvement, Endora remained a target of Richard's relentless pursuit of justice. After the guilty verdict, she received a harsher sentence than any of the other doctors in the practice: house arrest for the first year, and then probation for another four or five years. She lost her medical license for five years, as well as her ability to work at any place that billed Medicare. By that time, she had given birth to the baby she conceived while being prosecuted: a girl, whom she named Fancy Free. The baby's father was long gone, probably the smartest character in this whole story, if not the best father. He had the brains to get away from Endora as fast as he could.

When Endora lost her income, Richard began to give her money. Meanwhile, Natasha, who was no fool, got wise to the situation and started spending money to get even. Richard, now fifty-four, found himself calling his forty-two-year-old brother Lucas back in Missouri for help. We had plenty of money, so Lucas helped his brother for about a year, never knowing the full story about Endora and the prosecution until that phone call in Kansas City in 1998. Then it became necessary for Lucas to overcome his embarrassment and explain the situation to me.

He hung up the phone. "You're not going to believe what I have to tell you."

Lucas had just found out from Richard that his mistress, Endora, had a daughter of her own who had just turned two years old and, by the way, Endora was now seven months pregnant with Richard's baby.

"Lucas, something is very wrong here. How does a thirty-eight-year-old doctor get pregnant by a fifty-four-year-old lawyer by accident? Someone wanted this baby. Either she's trapping him, or he needs a way to finally work up the guts to leave his wife."

But he had already left his wife. Around Thanksgiving of that year, Richard had told Natasha about the baby and gone to live with Endora. He returned for Thanksgiving, but a few phone calls from Endora, along with Natasha's insistence on referring to the baby as "the devil's seed," quickly ended things. He and Endora were now a family.

We decided, together, that before sending any more assistance Lucas should go to Alabama. If he witnessed the situation firsthand, we could perhaps better understand Richard, and make a more informed decision on how best to help him and his family. The next week Lucas boarded a plane to Alabama. The evening of his arrival he called me, in total shock at the mess Richie had gotten himself into. Yes, he now went by the name "Richie." I've never been sure why, but it was just as well that his name changed because everything, and I mean everything, in his life had changed.

During his visit, Lucas saw for himself Endora's severe emotional problems. A passing stranger would notice that this woman was disturbed. The apartment they lived in was filthy, and Fancy Free ran all over the place without anyone watching or caring for her. Endora and Richie just sat at the table and chain smoked as they told Lucas their story. Endora made clear to Lucas her total lack of remorse for her fraud, even blaming Richie for her predicament right in front of him.

Lucas learned only that day about Richie's prosecution of Endora, and that she was under house arrest. When I heard, I was flabbergasted that he would become involved in any way with someone he had prosecuted. Richie rationalized Endora's blaming him by claiming that he had been too tough in her prosecution, the other doctors had gotten off with a slap on the hand. This was definitely not the Richard that we knew. Meanwhile, his estranged wife was threatening to go to the newspapers with the story of his relationship with Endora if he didn't come back to her.

That kind of ethics scandal could bring down the entire prosecutor's office. Richie had thought it best to resign, ostensibly so that if Natasha did go to the papers his colleagues would not be affected. Later we would learn that his relationship with Endora had begun earlier than they had let on, and his resignation was probably only a way to save his own rear end. Either way, neither Endora nor Richie had a job.

Endora shared everything with Lucas: her childhood, alcoholism, and depression, even her three abortions. So why did Richie choose to be with her? Lust, maybe? Sexual addiction? Or perhaps, in his arrogant way, he thought that he could save Endora, fix her broken emotional state, make her whole again.

Lucas tried to talk sense into Richie over dinner. He suggested that Richie come back to Missouri to stay with us and visit the rest of the family. He'd seen or spoken to them very little since an argument at his son Bert's graduation from the Air Force Academy five years earlier, partly at the insistence of the other controlling woman in his life, Natasha. (He had, however, called Lucas whenever he needed financial advice regarding a case.) Lucas even offered to hook Richie up with some good job interviews, if any worked out, he could move back to Missouri for good. Above all, Lucas stressed that Richie needed to get out of his relationship with Endora. She was severely ill, and all the love Richie could give would never heal her. Quite the opposite: her illness would drag him down, too. Lucas even suggested that destroying Richie might have been Endora's plan the entire time. A bad marriage didn't need to lead to affairs; there were other options. Richie could divorce Natasha if things were beyond repair, come home to Missouri, get a good job, and then send support to his family and to Endora's new baby.

No dice. Richie was deeply insulted by the suggestion that Endora had set him up. He professed his love for her and his certainty that she felt the same way. His ego prevented him from believing that a woman would be with him just to get even.

Of course, our suggestion that Endora had set this whole scenario up was pretty presumptuous on our part. But considering what Lucas saw, the little information we had been given about her, and what we knew about Richie's past, what would any rational person suspect? How *do* a thirty-eight year old doctor and a fifty-four year old lawyer conceive a child by accident? Why would a woman who has had three abortions suddenly decide, at the worst time in her life, to have two babies in a little more than two years? Did Fancy Free exist to keep her out of jail? Was the new baby intended to keep Richie from returning to his family? Did she seek him out hoping to get payback for her legal problems? How could he be stupid enough to get involved with a criminal? Did he need sex that badly? Did he hope their baby would give him the courage to leave his wife? Those unanswered questions aroused suspicion in us from the first moment that Lucas met Endora.

Chapter Three

The good news was that Richie decided to take Lucas's advice and come home for Christmas. The bad news: he was bringing Endora and Fancy Free with him. Lucas expressed his displeasure with that scenario, but we agreed to welcome them into our home nonetheless. Back in Missouri, Lucas did his best to prepare the rest of the family. He knew the shock they were in for, because the situation was so out of character for the Richard we all knew. We had to sit our girls down and prepare them to have these guests in our home, including a two-year old. Lindsay was fifteen, Nikki twelve, and Julia eight, they were very close; Nikki and Julia even chose to sleep in the same room. Lucas knew our girls would fall in love with Fancy Free, and we wanted to avoid the pain of loss for them down the road.

The girls and I spent the next few shopping days getting seven or eight Christmas presents for Fancy Free, including dolls and stuffed animals. Lucas had noticed that Endora's maternity clothes were pretty worn out and ill fitting, so we made sure to include gifts of that nature, too.

Two nights before Christmas Eve 1998, at around 8:30 in the evening, we answered a knock at our front door.

There stood Richie, Endora, and the precious Fancy Free. At first she was shy, hiding behind her mom. She didn't know what to make of all of us. (Little did we know that her clinging to Endora would be the only normal mother daughter bonding we would ever witness between them.) Two-year old Fancy Free was beautiful, with butter cream skin and jet-black hair with baby curls everywhere, dark eyes, large plump cheeks, and full lips. Exotic like her mother, and clearly not the daughter of a Caucasian man, a fact that Richie would later confirm, and that would come into play as we watched her grow.

It took less than an hour for Fancy Free to attach herself to our girls. She fell in love with them and they with her. Lucas and I tried to keep our distance, but it was no use: we were instantly smitten. She needed someone to cling to, to show her love and attention, to give her discipline and direction. After her initial shyness wore off, we saw a dominating and commanding personality who was very smart and unusually independent, likely from having to take care of herself most of the time, or perhaps she was just imitating her overbearing mom.

Richie and Endora pretty much ignored Fancy Free the whole time and let us take care of her. And she wanted nothing to do with them, choosing to be with the girls or me every minute. That was fine with us, we knew that Fancy Free had never experienced anything close to a normal family life before. The girls treated her like a sister, and she opted to sleep with them for the entire stay.

Endora and I spent a lot of time talking when Lucas took Richie out to meet some of his attorney friends. In spite of all I'd heard, I liked her and had to remind myself (or be reminded by Lucas) that she was a habitual liar. It struck me that she didn't look like a doctor, with her heavy eye makeup and a demeanor that wasn't exactly intellectual. I found myself wondering if her whole medical career hadn't been a scam. During these conversations, Endora revealed her past to me, as well as the story of how she met Richie. She was baffled by the fact that we had taken them into our home and were trying to help them out.

"That's just what family does, Endora," I said.

She looked at me with confusion. That wasn't what her family did. I could tell she was waiting for the flip side: *Now what am I going to have to do for you?*

They were with us for about nine days, maybe two weeks. Richie had several interviews with a large law firm in Missouri. We could tell he hoped to get a job offer so that he, Endora, and Fancy Free could move back permanently. One problem: Endora was not so keen on the idea. They spent several days going off by themselves, who knows where, to discuss their future. Fancy Free was always left with us.

The firm did offer Richie a job, but he wouldn't start until February, giving them time to go back to Alabama and pack, and time to figure out what to do with Endora's mother, Iris. Fancy Free was distraught. She wanted to stay with us. It was the first instance of a pattern: she has never shown a single sign of missing Endora and Richie when they went away; in fact, she would grow upset when they returned home. That first time, she was consoled only when we told her that they would be coming back to see us in a few weeks.

Chapter Four

In early February 1999, Richie, Endora, Fancy Free, and Endora's mother, Iris, returned to Missouri. They planned to stay with us until they found a place to live. Richie and Endora had shared various stories concerning Iris's mental health, so her presence concerned us. But Richie had convinced Endora to move only by agreeing to bring Iris with them. Endora's mother provided a connection to Alabama.

As soon as we met Iris, Lucas and I worried about leaving our children alone with her. She looked like an older version of Endora, with hair styled exactly the same but solid gray. She slurred her speech and was often off balance and glassy-eyed. She reminded me of the Indian in *One Flew Over the Cuckoo's Nest*. While carrying her bags upstairs, Lindsay saw one that was filled with prescription pill bottles.

After Richard and his brood arrived, our two older daughters stayed with friends as often as possible and the youngest, Julia, slept with us in our bedroom with the door closed and locked. When the other two were at home, they slept in our bedroom as well.

Meanwhile, Lucas's family had decided to help give Richie half a chance at starting over. A few days after they arrived, his sister Nancy, Maria's twin, found a house for Richie and Endora to rent in the same area of Missouri that several of us lived in. It was safe, well kept, though on a busy street and in need of cleaning. The house was a tough sell, and the landlord jumped at the chance to rent to a doctor and a lawyer. Lucas put down a deposit. Richie was pleased with the little home; Endora was not. Nancy, Maurene (another sister), and their mom went to work cleaning up the place while Lucas, Richie, and Endora headed out to buy a refrigerator.

Everyone put up a brave front, but not one of us thought Richie's new life with Endora was a good idea. No one in the family had been close to Natasha, but they were Catholic and didn't exactly approve of Richie's leaving his wife and children for the woman with whom he'd been having an affair. Though we discussed these things amongst ourselves, it was the family way to act positively in front of Richie and Endora. After all, a new baby was on the way.

Once the fridge was delivered, the move could begin. It was a joke from the minute we looked inside the U-Haul that had been sitting in front of our house for the past several days they stayed with us. Richie brought nothing; he had left his family with only the clothes on his back. Endora, on the other hand, had packed everything that she had ever owned, and possibly some things she stole.

Remember Endora's five thousand square foot house? Well, once she was forced to sell that and move into a small apartment, she had put everything into storage. Their new house was small, only nine hundred square feet. So when they moved to Missouri they packed everything from her little apartment into the U-Haul, and then went to the storage unit and packed up the rest. They had rented the largest truck U-Haul had, and it was filled to the top. By the time we emptied that truck into that nine hundred square foot house, there was barely any room to walk. Did I say, "emptied"? We couldn't even come close, so off Lucas and Richie went to another storage facility to rent a unit for all of Endora's junk.

Endora had obviously not gone through anything, ever. She had files from her practice; clothes that would never fit her again and were out of style anyway; and furniture that was falling apart. She apparently liked to shop for antique furniture that needed to be refinished, but as with everything else in her life, this hobby was over before it started. So pieces that could have been beautiful were scratched, or missing a leg or an inlay. Everything had been packed without care; they must have taken the dishes right off the kitchen table and thrown them into the U-Haul. Coffee rings and jelly smears still sullied them. Clothes were stained, ashtrays and wastebaskets filthy, pots and pans unwashed. *Just pack up and let's go.*

At the end of moving day, after Lucas had paid for the truck rental, storage rental, advance rent on the house, and new refrigerator, we lay in bed and told each other it had been a hopeless waste of time.

We had little contact with Richie and Endora for the next several days. They needed time to get organized, and to find a doctor, as Endora was due to deliver the baby any day. Not having medical insurance, they were sure to throw this expense our way. They also needed to find some sort of institution for Iris. Fed up, we just needed to be away from them for a while. Watching their disorganization and dysfunction firsthand wore us down. And Fancy Free had needed to be watched during the few days Richie and Endora spent preparing for their move. They would have left her alone at our house with Iris; even after all of the awful stories they had told us about Iris's mistreatment of Endora and her siblings. We thought of leaving one of our daughters to care for Fancy Free, but that would have meant leaving her alone with Iris. So when Lucas and I went out, we sent our children to friends' homes and took Fancy Free with us. If Lucas were helping Richie, I would watch Fancy Free. If I needed to help Endora, Lucas would care for her. Sometimes when both of us were needed we would find a place where Lucas's mom could sit with her. Now, the four of them were alone together in that cramped, overstuffed house.

When they had first arrived at our house, right after the initial introductions, Richie and Endora had made sure that we understood Endora's background. Richie wanted us to know that he knew Endora had problems. He felt that all of them stemmed from the dysfunctional upbringing she suffered at the hands of her mother. He thought, if Endora were surrounded by a loving and caring extended family, she would begin to see what life was really all about. What they didn't realize was that every time they chose to leave Fancy Free alone with Iris, they were saying, "We know this isn't a wise decision but it's the kind of care Endora got and Endora survived." We saw from day one that they would always come first, their children second.

Chapter Five

Joel was born on February 10, 1999. His given name was Joseph, but since Richie already had a son named Joseph, he was called Joel. Their stay at the hospital was very short, as there was no insurance. Joel looked just like one of Richie's other sons. I just couldn't remember which one, as it had been years since I had seen any of them. There was no doubt he was a Howitt. He had that mouth the men of the family all possess. Based on what I had seen of Endora, a part of me had wondered if maybe the baby wasn't really Richie's. Now that I knew it was, I have to admit I had trouble wanting to be around Joel. He reminded me so much of Richie, for whom, by this time, I had no respect. Every time I looked at Joel all I could see was Richie. The truth is, I avoided being around Joel at first because I felt guilty. I couldn't feel the love for him that I had felt for every other child in my life.

In almost no time, it became clear that I had better get over these feelings because Joel and Fancy Free were going to need Lucas and I. Richie would say things like "Endora is not bonding well with the baby." When they came over, Richie would try to act like the perfect dad, feeding and changing the baby. But no one was fooled. He lacked patience and was awkward and rough with Joel when things like diaper changing didn't go smoothly. Still, while he was trying, Endora just ignored her new baby. This was when we began to see that the children would never receive proper care. If Endora couldn't even pretend to bond with her own child in front of family, it was no great leap to imagine the lack of attention given to them at home when no one was watching.

During this period I would pick up Fancy Free during the day to bring her over to our house, where she could play with the girls after school and we could make sure she had a decent meal. Afterward, she always cried as soon as I pulled into the driveway at Richie and Endora's house. She would beg me to let her come back home with me. When I walked out the front door, leaving her behind, I would count to five, turn around, and there she would be, standing in the front picture window. She had to climb up on the couch and push the aluminum blinds out of the way, but there she would be. As I pulled out of the drive-way she pounded on the window and cried. After a couple of times I noticed the blinds were barely hanging on the windows anymore.

At the end of February, Richie started his new job at the law firm in Missouri. That's when the problems really began. I remember having a conversation with Endora while she was still staying at our house. She had expressed concerns about staying home with Fancy Free and the new baby, who had not then arrived yet. She said that she did not like the idea of staying home; she wanted a career and wanted someone else to take care of the kids. As we talked I thought Endora grasped that a career was just not possible right then: Richie had a good enough job to support them both, and she was not going to be able to make enough money to justify paying a babysitter. She could not work as a doctor, I argued, so why shouldn't she just stay home and enjoy some time with her kids? Down the road, she would have time to work on getting her medical license back and having a career. I did not sugarcoat staying home though, I explained to her that she was used to a career where she was respected and patted on the back, and stay-at-home moms don't get that kind of respect. When she worked long hours, her paycheck used to reflect it. She'd never earn overtime playing the role of a homemaker. I told her that it would be the hardest job she would ever do, even though most people treat it like anyone can do it and do it well. This woman had put herself through medical school and had borne the responsibility of a doctor. Now she looked at me and smirked. I thought to myself, *you have no idea, those poor children.* I had no idea how right I was.

One evening shortly after Joel was born, I got a call from a woman stating she was Joel's pediatrician. She said, "Are you related to Endora Howitt?" I explained to her that I was related to Joel, not elaborating and explaining that Endora was not a Howitt. She just liked to act as if she was. Richie still had not divorced his first wife. Anyway, the doctor went on to ask if I was available to go over to Endora's house and "check on the baby." She said that Endora had called, frantic. It seemed Joel would not stop crying and Endora was at the end of her rope. I'm not sure what she told the doctor, but the doctor was convinced that Endora was going to hurt the baby. I told the doctor that I would go over immediately. I called Endora and told her that I was on my way. I told her to just leave the room, since she was so upset. Just get as far away from Joel as she could, and "don't touch him."

When I got there, Joel was screaming. She had him sitting in a pumpkin seat on top of the kitchen table. Endora paced like a madwoman, with her usual dark eye makeup and black clothes, letting go of her cigarette only long enough to clutch at her messy hair. The smoke in the room from her puffing on one cigarette after another, was enough to make the baby sick alone. It was obvious that Endora had been crying. She paced the room, puffing away, ashes falling wherever, stopping only to grab her hair by the roots and look furiously at Joel. I wasn't sure how to handle her. I wasn't even sure she remembered that I called.

"Endora, I'm here to help you. Can I go see to Joel?"

"God, yes, please. Help me."

So I walked over and picked him up. He sat in a puddle of his own urine, so wet his diaper had to have been useless for hours. I took him to a bedroom to change him. Fancy Free followed me. Honestly, if he hadn't already been in such bad shape, I would never have put him down anywhere in that filthy house. It was apparent that no attempts to clean had occurred, though they had lived there for a month. As soon as I changed Joel, he stopped crying. It was like turning off the radio.

"Fancy Free, can you watch Joel for just a minute?" I spread a baby blanket on the floor and laid Joel on it. I explained to her that she should not pick him up, just sit next to him.

I went back into the kitchen, where Endora just sat, still puffing. I brought Joel's pumpkin seat over to the sink and started to clean it out. After a while, Endora spoke.

"I'm starting to feel a little better."

"Endora, would you like me to take the kids home with me?"

"No, Richie will get upset."

Apparently, Richie demanded a home-cooked meal when he returned from work every day, one with sauces and gravy, the whole bit.

"He knows I'm not like that, but that's what he got with his wife."

Of course, I was thinking, *so everything Natasha did wasn't so bad*, but I kept my mouth shut and let Endora talk for a while. She talked about how Richie didn't understand her unhappiness. He expected her to take care of the kids, at least attempt to clean the house, do some laundry, and have a meal on the table when he came home from work.

"No one could do all of that," Endora said.

Now, there was a whole world of women who did "all of that" all the time, and most of them weren't very happy about it. It could get extremely boring. But what had she thought being at home with two young children would entail? She was not taking care of the kids, the house was a mess, and no meal was in the works, what exactly had she done all day?

Apparently, Fancy Free had been an unusually easy

baby, and Endora had felt an attachment to her that she never felt to Joel, partly because Fancy Free was her spitting image, and partly because Joel had been conceived for manipulative purposes in the first place. If he wasn't helping her keep Richie, Endora wanted no part of him. At that point, she may also have been suffering from postpartum depression.

I tried to guide her back to the kids, as delicately as possible. After all, I was dealing with an unstable woman, a doctor who might not take kindly to a less-educated woman instructing her on what to do.

"Endora, do you think Joel will be hungry soon? When's the last time you fed him? Has Fancy Free eaten dinner? Endora, do you think I should take the kids home with me for the night?"

"No. Joel is fine. Don't worry, Richie will be home soon; he's much better with the baby than I am."

That didn't exactly put my mind at ease. "Is Joel on formula?"

"Yes."

Here's where it really got hard. I needed to state the obvious without pissing her off. "Endora, I know that you are a doctor, but sometimes when a baby is crying we don't think rationally."

She gave a little laugh. "Yeah."

"Endora, if the feedings are going well, he is going to fill his diapers more often." "Yeah." Another little laugh.

"If he starts crying or screaming, you just start with the things you know a baby wants and needs, like food, a diaper change, or just wrapping him in his receiving blanket."

"Yeah, they do like being wrapped up tight. Why do you suppose that is?"

Somehow, this hint of inquisitiveness was encouraging.

"Well, I suppose it's because they are pretty used to the tight quarters of the womb."

She thought for a moment. "Yeah, that does make sense."

We talked for a little while and she began to relax a little, at least, she stopped pacing and chain-smoking. She assured me that Richie was on his way, and calmly asked me to leave. I asked her to promise me that as soon as she felt herself start to lose it in the future, she would call me. I suggested that she talk with Richie about letting Lucas and I keep both the kids for a weekend, so that she and Richie could have some time alone. A little sleep could do a lot for a person's sanity, or so I hoped. She said that she would love to take me up on that, but she'd have to work on Richie.

"He feels we should be enjoying our babies."

Yeah, that's why most people have them.

Less than a month after our relationship with Endora and Richie began, it was abundantly clear that nothing about it was going to be normal.

Chapter Six

Within a week, Endora called to see if the kids could come and spend the weekend at our house. Lucas was out of town, but the girls were around, so I said yes. I figured the girls could play with Fancy Free, and I could spend some time with Joel. Richie and Endora had told us that Joel had stomach problems. He was crying a lot and not sleeping through the night. It sounded to me like colic. Richie said Endora was giving Joel some type of medicine, so I hoped to find out what it was and whether it was necessary. Any time the rest of the family was around him, he was fine.

When it was time for bed, Nikki and Julia took Fancy Free with them. Not wanting Lucas to come home and lie down on the baby, or the baby to fall off the bed, I set up a place on the floor next to my side of the bed with blankets and pillows. At his age, he wasn't going to move much, and I could be close by in case he started to cry. He went down around 11:00. He cried and woke me up at 3:00 a.m. I fed him a bottle and put him back down. Lucas had arrived home from his trip by then, and was shocked that we were taking care of Joel overnight at such a young age. Lying in bed, we talked of sending one of our newborns off overnight, and we couldn't imagine it, not even to stay with our parents, unless it was an emergency.

Monday morning, Joel woke up at 7:00 a.m., just as the rest of us were getting ready for the weekday. We had given Joel no medicine that weekend. He woke up like clockwork for his feedings, and was happy after each one. Endora didn't even send any medicine over, prompting me to wonder: Did she not want me to know what she was giving him, or did she just want things to be tough on us to see if we could handle it any better than she could?

When I took the kid's home that Monday morning, I sat down with Endora to discuss things. Lucas and I wanted to make sure that Joel wasn't being given medication that he didn't need. When I told Endora how things had gone, I could tell she knew we were suspicious about why he was being medicated. So she started drilling me about exactly what I had done with him. I told her that we let him stay up until he was showing signs of tiredness. I told her that with my first daughter, I focused too hard on getting her on my schedule. With the next baby, we tried just letting her be the guide for the first several months. That plan ended up working better and faster. Before we knew it, the baby was sleeping through the night. The baby might not always be ready for bed at 8:00, but when she slept for six hours or more at a time, it gave Lucas and me a little peace.

Endora wasn't impressed. She wanted to know exactly what we had done with Joel. I told her we fed him and then put him down at 11:00. I told her that I wrapped him tight in a receiving blanket, just like I had shown her, and put him down on his stomach. Suddenly she came unglued, ranting about doctors saying that putting babies on their stomachs is what they think is causing SIDS. I just let her talk, pacing again, addressing me as if I was a total failure for not being up on the latest details of pediatric research. After she completed her lecture on baby care, it was my turn.

"Endora, it's not easy for me to talk to you right now, because you're speaking to me as a doctor, not as a mother who has to get up every night and feed and hold her crying baby. You may be a lot more educated than I am, but you know what? I've got a lot more experience dealing with babies. Maybe that's the difference between what they call 'book learning' and 'street learning.'"

She seemed to be listening, so I continued. "Maybe you didn't experience this with Fancy Free, but pediatricians will tell you a lot of things about when to add food to the diet, when to take them off formula, and everything else. Endora, every baby is different. The doctor doesn't wake up in the middle of the night listening to the crying and feeling the frustration building. So you have to make a decision: Do I lay this baby on his stomach so that he feels safe and comfortable and cries less, and take a chance with the small risk of this SIDS thing, or do I listen to what the doctor says and let my frustration build so much that I would consider doing something criminal to my baby? Yes, Endora, *criminal*. Which do you think would be worse? A week ago, your pediatrician had to call me because she was so worried about your frustration level. Endora, how often do you think a doctor takes the time to call a relative and ask her to check on a baby?"

"Not very often."

"You've got that right. So your behavior over the phone must have had this doctor very concerned for Joel's safety." She backed off a little from her anger about the SIDS risk. So I went on to explain to her that these issues would come up a lot with directions from the pediatrician. She needed to remember that they were mostly just suggestions and that every baby, including Joel, was different.

"You have to adjust to the needs of your child, Endora." Then I got up and left.

After that incident, we didn't hear from them as much. Occasionally we would call to see if Fancy Free could come over, or Richie would call and ask us to watch the kids for a couple of hours so that he could go and shop at the base without the kids. Endora was never happy to be left alone, since they had only one car. Richie had to take it to work each day, so she was left with two children and no way to get out of the house. Richie would often call Lucas at work to ask for financial help. He was paying a huge amount in alimony to Natasha, and Lucas could tell that he was starting to get depressed. Endora's unhappiness, his attempts to make a good impression at work, coming home to deal with two babies, it was all taking its toll. His marriage to Natasha had been quite different. Richie had not been burdened with any responsibility for their children, much the opposite, in fact. Natasha had treated him as though he had no business trying to care for the boys. She had done all the cleaning, cooking, laundry, household errands, and shuffling of the kids to various activities. Now Richie finally saw the upside to that situation.

Every once in a while, Richie came home from work to find that Endora had been drinking. Richie claimed that Endora had not previously consumed alcohol during their relationship. The behavior was a new problem for him because it was more than just a few drinks a fight would inevitably ensue, as Endora was supposed to be a recovering alcoholic. Richie would then leave to cool off. Then Endora would call our house to see if we had heard from Richie. Lucas first found out about the drinking from these calls. He could tell by talking to Endora. When Lucas confronted Richie, Richie confirmed his suspicion.

So now we knew that not only were the children not being taken care of, but their mother was also getting drunk while at home alone with them.

One evening, Lucas and Lindsay, our oldest daughter, were home by themselves. The phone rang, and Lucas picked up to hear Fancy Free's three-year-old voice. "Lucas, come get me."

Lucas could hear Endora screaming at her in the background. "Fancy Free, you get off that phone!"

Fancy Free just repeated, "Lucas, you better come and get me." Lucas handed Lindsay the phone and told her to keep Fancy Free on the line as long as she could while he got into the car with his cell phone. Racing over to Endora's house, Lucas tried to get a hold of Richie. He failed to find him, but Richie did arrive home before Lucas got there, perhaps Fancy Free had called him, too. Richie called Lucas in his car to tell him not to come over: he had everything under control.

Earlier that night, Richie had gotten home from work and Endora was once again drunk. Enraged, Richie left the house on foot to take a walk and cool down. I would have given him credit for that, if it hadn't meant leaving the kids alone with a drunk. He could have put the kids in the car and just come over to our house. Or stayed in denial and taken the kids to McDonald's. Let Endora stay home alone and worry about being abandoned.

When I got home, Lucas had returned, and he told me the story. I couldn't believe the severe dysfunction present in that household, or that Fancy Free was intelligent enough, at three years old, to call our house by herself. Not possible. That meant that her mother had dialed our number and told Fancy Free to tell us to come and get her. Then, during the phone call, Endora started screaming at her little girl. When you're three years old, and you do what your mother tells you, she's not supposed to start ranting at you. This was probably the same type of behavior Endora grew up with from Iris. Which explained a lot.

Chapter Seven

Even with things less than perfect with Endora and the baby, Richie still proceeded with his divorce. He had not seen or heard from his sons since the separation from Natasha, and probably feared facing them after what he had done. He was willing to give his wife whatever she wanted just to get the divorce over with, even if it meant never seeing his sons again. He didn't agree to this out of guilt or sorrow for cheating on his wife and leaving his family. He gave up everything simply because Endora insisted that they get married, and that couldn't happen until he permanently severed the tie with his former family. He gave his ex-wife everything, including his pension from the Air Force.

No one blamed Natasha; he had caused her and their sons so much pain she had every right to ask for everything. Richie was an attorney, he didn't need to give in so easily. The pension was good, but his first family would never be able to survive off it without drastically changing their way of life. So he agreed to an additional monthly allowance he would never be able to pay. If he did, he wouldn't be able to provide for family number two. If he didn't come up with the money each month, he would be considered a deadbeat dad and the authorities would come after him. So he had set himself up for failure either way. The amazing part was that he acted blind to the problem. Why? Now Endora was happy. As she saw it, he was entirely rid of his first family now. She never intended to let him send money at all.

Richie and Endora got married in September 1999. They didn't just go off to the courthouse or a justice of the peace. No, Endora had to go the whole nine yards. She planned a wedding ceremony in a beautiful building within a large park. This building displays tropical flowers and plants throughout the year, with a man-made stream and waterfall. Endora wore an elaborate white gown with a neckline that revealed most of her large bosom, and insisted on a dress for Fancy Free that was almost as elaborate as her own. It must have cost a few hundred dollars, but its white skirt was black within an hour of Fancy Free putting it on. Even baby Joel wore a suit.

The whole ordeal was a joke, and we made quite a few colorful comments under our breaths as it unfolded. Guess who ended up paying for this joke? Endora and Richie had planned a small reception at a restaurant, but neglected to make arrangements to pay in advance. After we arrived, Richie pulled Lucas aside and told him we'd have to pick up the tab.

Shortly after that, they enrolled Fancy Free in a pre-school that they couldn't afford. It had to be a private Montessori school. They still had only one car, but Endora talked Richie into letting her keep it during the day. He was an attorney at one of the largest law firms in Missouri, and he had to take the bus to work. I'm sure his employer was not impressed. Richie called Lucas several times to ask if he would pay Fancy Free's tuition. We couldn't believe that he could actually ask us to do this. We didn't even send our own children to that type of preschool. They sent her anyway, and though we didn't write any checks for her tuition, the fact that we paid all of their other bills helped make it possible. But within a couple of months Endora pulled Fancy Free out, claiming the teacher was "doing inappropriate stuff to her." I couldn't help thinking, *what could possibly be more inappropriate than her living conditions with you?* But I kept my mouth shut. I now believe this teacher may have been ready to make a report of some sort to the Division of Family Services regarding what she was observing when Fancy Free arrived at school. This would happen again when Fancy Free began elementary school; in fact, every school of hers that I have been in contact with has filed a report to social services.

On Christmas Eve in the year 2000, everyone in Lucas's family came over to our house. Endora and Richie showed up late, as usual. Fancy Free appeared with a very strange, uneven haircut. When I asked Endora about it, she told me that Fancy Free had gotten a hold of some scissors and cut her own hair. It occurred to me that she must have had an awful lot of time by herself, as this wasn't just the little snip of the bangs that most kids do when they decided to try that stunt. It was all over her head. Endora expressed concern that it was a warning sign of self-mutilation. What mother in her right mind would think of that, just because her three-year old went at her own hair with a scissors?

After that Christmas, Lucas and I decided that we needed to be away from this whole situation for a while. This was difficult as our girls often asked if the kids could come over and play. We would always try to sidetrack our girls without revealing to much about the turmoil we knew was involved in Richie and Endora' relationship. Still, Lucas continued to pay most of their bills. Richie called him at the bank at least weekly requesting money for rent, food, and Joel's medical bills. They'd now been in Missouri for more than a year, Joel was almost one, Fancy Free three, and their situation was in decline. Richie admitted to Lucas that Endora had seen a doctor and been diagnosed with depression and bipolar disorder. She was taking medication, but it caused her to gain a lot of weight, leading only to deeper depression. So she started to self-medicate, she was very persuasive, and had friends in the medical profession, so no prescription was unattainable. The problems in their relationship just worsened. With two young children in the picture, and unimaginable stress in the house, Richie was reaching the end of his rope.

Chapter Eight

In March 2001 Endora was arrested for shoplifting from Target. When I got the call from Lucas on my cell phone, I was on my way home from Julia's indoor softball game. Julia, our youngest, was ten years old. I coached the team and always had a blast with the kids. But that day my excitement faded when Lucas told me that Endora had gone shopping in the only car they had and left the kids with Richie. She had gotten arrested and called Richie to come get her out of jail. Having no way to do this without a car, he of course called Lucas, who went over to pick up Richie and the kids. He brought the kids back to our house, where I watched them while Lucas and Richie went to the jail to bail Endora out. Later, Richie came over to pick up the kids, very grateful and very embarrassed. We never heard any remorse, embarrassment, or "thank you" from Endora.

After that incident, Richie discussed with Lucas the possibility of he and kids moving into our home. Lucas didn't want that, knowing it would mean having to deal with Endora. I didn't want it either, knowing that Richie was only trying to save his career and I would become the kid's nanny. I knew what kind of hours Richie was capable of working. Lucas was the same way. And Richie was having a hard time building his stature at the firm, since he'd been a criminal prosecutor, he was unfamiliar with corporate law and often had to spend time on research that couldn't be billed to the clients. I'd been responsible for our children twenty-four hours a day, seven days a week for years. It's one thing to do it for your own husband and children. I love my family, so I put up with it. There was no way I was going to put up with it for Richie and Endora.

Besides, Richie and I had very different opinions about parenting and discipline. Lucas and I had successfully raised three daughters without hitting, spanking, or even much yelling. We never really used the "time-out method," but we would send them to their rooms if we were approaching the ends of our ropes. We were very firm and didn't back down or send mixed messages. Mostly we tried to use positive reinforcement to encourage the behavior we wanted, instead of waiting for bad behavior and then using negative reinforcement to extinguish it.

Richie, on the other hand, was a disciplinarian. He acted as if the children were soldiers and he was their commanding officer, making a big deal about things that simply didn't matter. He insisted they finish every bite of food on their plates, no matter what. Everything was black and white, with no room for compassion or complication. There was just no way I was going to deal with that on a daily basis. I was going to raise the kids or Richie was; we'd never do it together. By that time our daughters were seventeen, fourteen, and ten. I was having a great time watching them play soccer, tennis, softball, dance;

and just enjoy being around their friends. In addition to coaching Julia's softball team, I was playing tennis myself, and had even gone back to school. Now Richie expected me to give all that up because he was having a midlife crisis. I suppose I should have been more concerned about Joel and Fancy Free, but my focus was on Richie and all the stupid decisions he had made. We had provided for him for almost two years and that still wasn't enough. I was angry.

Two months later, in May 2001, Endora was caught shoplifting again. This time she had Fancy Free with her, so she wasn't sent to jail. She learned quickly, and in the future made sure one of the kids was always with her when she did something illegal. Unless you've been violent, the police won't take you to jail because if they can't get a hold of the father, then they have to call the Division of Family Services to care for the kids. They don't want to take children away from their mothers for petty offenses. The situation also provided an education for Joel and Fancy Free, who, as we would soon see, were learning to steal and to lie about it.

Richie, meanwhile, knew now that it was just a matter of time before he would lose his job. He had managed to keep it this long only because of the friendships and business relationship Lucas had with the firm. Richie continually had to leave work in the middle of the day to take care of the kids. Neighbors would call him after seeing them playing in the middle of the street, or he would call home and not get an answer for hours, Endora was out of control. Richie's checking account showed up on the overdraft sheet every morning. This report would ultimately go to the board of directors, and it didn't look so good for the brother of the president of the bank to be always overdrawing his account. Lucas decided it was time to drop in on Endora and Richie.

Lucas drove over in the middle of the day, in the middle of the week. Richie was home from work, a bad sign. The house was a disaster and the kids a mess. Lucas told his brother and sister-in-law that he was done; he would not give them another dime. He told them that we didn't want the kids to suffer and would do anything for them, even suggesting that they let us raise them. That way Richie and Endora could have time to get their lives together. Figure out if they should stay together or part ways.

Endora became very upset. Lucas explained that their landlord had called the bank, and it was over. He had told the landlord he would not pay any more of the rent. Within two months they'd be living on the streets. Lucas looked at Endora. "Is that really what you want for your kids?" Endora looked back at Lucas and said, "You think I'm a bad mother, don't you?" Lucas gave her no answer, and was kicked out of the house and called several colorful names in the process. Talk about biting the hand that has fed you.

By June 2001 Endora was bouncing checks all over town, still using the account at Lucas's bank. So Lucas contacted his brother and told him to take the checkbook and all the unused checks to work with him. That way Endora couldn't mess with the account. Richie did so, but that didn't stop Endora. She just went to different bank branches and mentioned her last name. When the teller saw who she was, they would give her a temporary check, the kind you use when you're opening a new account and are waiting for your checks to be printed. When Lucas figured this out and shut it down, she found a way to use the Internet to get it done.

Meanwhile, the checks Endora was bouncing were made out mostly to a local grocery store, Foodmart. Lucas's other brother, Mark, just happened to be employed by this chain for more than twenty years. Why would she go to that particular grocery store when the town had several others? It seemed obvious to me: Endora was no longer happy with trying to ruin Richie's life; she was now bent on hurting the rest of the family in the process. She was able to flash her last name at both the bank and the grocery store and get what she wanted, and at the same time put both Lucas and Mark in precarious situations. The two brothers, however, were not as fooled by her as Richie had been and refused to let that happen. Lucas closed out the bank account and Mark let his superiors know that they should treat Endora like any other individual who writes bad checks.

In October 2001, Richie finally lost his job. Now neither he nor Endora was working. Nor was either employable. Endora had lost her license to practice medicine because of the Medicare fraud, and besides, one look at her and any intelligent human being could tell something was not right. Richie had been forced to resign from a previous job, and now had been fired from his most recent job. Who would hire either of them once a background check was completed?

What went on in that home from October until the beginning of December must have been horrible. What must it have been like to possess the amount of education these two had and not have been able to find work? There was no money to fall back on. Their utilities were turned on and off. They knew the streets were only days away. They had two young children who didn't understand any of this and were probably driving them nuts. And they had hurt each other so much by that point that they couldn't talk without arguing. Which meant that Richie avoided talking at all. To make matters worse, the holidays were closing in.

Chapter Nine

From this point on, the story is no longer about just a dysfunctional family. It is a story of societal dysfunction. Even I, who had refused to be Richie's kids' nanny, realized that something would have to be done to save those children from their own parents. I had begun talking with my sister-in-law Maria back in September. We were sitting and watching my middle daughter, Nikki, play in a high-school softball tournament. This tournament was about a hundred miles from our town, but only about thirty miles from where Maria lives. So Maria and her husband, Neal, had come to watch the games with me. Maria had spent time on the phone talking with her mom about Richie and his new family. All the Howitts were deeply concerned about the situation.

The conversation between Maria and me that day inevitably led to Richie. I told Maria that I had given it a lot of thought, and felt that it was only a matter of time before someone would have to step up and take responsibility for the children. I told her that I was not ready to take on two kids who were two and four years old. If I did, I would have to ask my own kids to give up a lot of their activities. That just didn't seem fair. But ignoring the situation didn't seem fair to Fancy Free and Joel. So I said that Lucas and I would be willing to take on Fancy Free, and if no one else in the family felt that they could take Joel in, that maybe we should consider putting him up for adoption. My reasoning was this: Fancy Free knew all of us and was old enough to remember us. Joel was so young he wouldn't even remember his sister. He was also very adoptable: only two, a male, with blond hair and blue eyes, and adorable. He was a blood relative and Fancy Free was not, but that didn't matter. I could not imagine taking on both kids, and to be honest, I still saw Richie every time I looked at his son.

Maria said that she understood my thinking, but that we could never give up Joel, as this would kill their mom, Joel's grandmother. I knew that she was right, so we just agreed to continue thinking about the situation and praying for answers. Maria and I had been very close ever since I was in college, when we two couples spent a lot of time together, and had been separated from each other only by our own children's activities. Now, Maria's boys were grown, and she and Neal were experiencing withdrawal from attending football and basketball games. So they started showing up to our girls' games, and our bond began to renew itself. Every time we were together our conversation naturally led to Joel and Fancy Free. Our concern for them grew daily. We started making inquiries to Family Services to see if they could help. Now, I was very naive about the social services agencies in this country. I thought that they were there to help children that their focus would be 100 percent on the well being of the child. How wrong was I?

Here begins the story of how the Division of Family Services really works. I had thought the abnormal behavior of Endora and Richie's family was bad, but it didn't compare to the dysfunction of the very institution intended to help them.

Chapter Ten

This point in the story is also where the light bulb finally turned on in Richie's head. It would still flicker from time to time, but deep down in his heart, he knew it was over. He knew he had totally screwed up. There was no turning back and no fixing the damage that had been inflicted. Pride had kept him from admitting what we all already knew: There was no fixing Endora, no fixing this family. This family never should have existed. He had allowed Endora into his life, back him into a corner, and now knew only to run away. He couldn't take it anymore, so he left. He just walked out the front door, again leaving a wife and kids without even packing a suitcase. He walked aimlessly for hours, finally ending up at his sister Nancy's front door. Nancy took him in, what else could she do? He was her brother; she loved him.

This was always my biggest problem with Richie: He had worked for one of the biggest and most prestigious law firms in Missouri. So he would have had access to their library. Being a lawyer doesn't make you an expert on every type of legal situation, but it did give him the wherewithal to research family law. To find out what his rights were, to help protect the children. But he never took the time. The thought probably never even entered his mind. So when he had enough he just got up and left. He saved himself, but left two innocent children with a mother he knew was severely mentally ill. Nancy didn't know what to do with him. She knew all that Lucas and I had been through with Endora. There was no way she could help Richie without facing the fact that she would have to contend with Endora. So she called Lucas.

At Nancy's, Lucas took Richie outside. "What is it you want me to do? What is it you want any of us to do? You wouldn't listen to me, and everything that I said would happen has now happened. You knew better than to show up at my doorstep, so now you have gone and involved Nancy so that one more family member can feel as bad as Rene and I have felt over this whole thing from the beginning." Richie literally begged for help, and Lucas's heart welled up with compassion for his brother. He was also concerned about the strain Richie would be placing on Nancy's marriage, so he gave in and agreed to help, only this time Richie received a list of things he had to be willing to do to get his life in order, or he would not be welcome in our home. Lucas informed him that the minute he suspected Richie wasn't working full time on those things, he would be out the door.

First, Richie had to file for divorce from Endora. He also had to attempt to reduce the exorbitant support payments he had agreed to give Natasha but couldn't afford. He was to declare bankruptcy. Finally, he needed to find work, even if it was at Burger King.

Richie came home with Lucas. He had hatched a plan to go back to school to become an over-the-road truck driver. That way he wouldn't really need a place to live; he could just travel and live out of his truck. He would never make the kind of money an attorney made, but he could make a decent living. Most important, he would be away from Endora and all his troubles. He could forget about his first wife and three sons. He could forget about walking out on them and never sending them any support. He could forget about Endora, and the two children he left to fend for themselves with a lunatic, one of them being his son. He believed that the money a truck driver made, with no other bills, would be enough for him to live on and to support Joel and Fancy Free. As though financial support would take care of them emotionally. He talked himself into believing that this plan would make him fiscally sound and be the answer to all of his and the kids' problems.

Even though Lucas knew that wasn't the answer, he saw hope in his brother's eyes, and a drive to try to improve his circumstances. Lucas told him that the plan was a start, but he still had to do everything on the list in order to remain in our home. First, he had to file for divorce from Endora and second, file an appeal regarding his first divorce. Richie had agreed to pay a monthly amount to his ex-wife that he could not afford even when he had been making ninety thousand dollars a year. Natasha had won his entire pension from the Air Force, which amounted to about thirty thousand dollars a year. She deserved that, but the additional monthly support he agreed to was just too much especially given Richie's dire financial circumstances. Natasha had, rightfully, been chasing after him.

So Lucas told him he had to file for a reduction, or he would always be considered a deadbeat dad. Richie agreed to all this, and to look for work, but Lucas had to stay on top of him daily like a parent with a child who won't do his homework.

Richie got busy right away finding out what it would take to be a truck driver, using our computer and working out of our finished basement. After several phone calls he found out that he would have to go to a facility in Indiana for training. Lucas would drive Richie there and get him set up in a hotel. The program didn't end until the first of the year, so Richie was going to miss Christmas. It was a three-week program, and since Richie had no money, Lucas agreed to pay for the school and living expenses. Knowing he wouldn't use it wisely, we didn't want to leave him with too much cash. The same thinking we would use with one of our kids. Endora had been all over Richie for money since he'd arrived at our house. She knew he had none, but figured he could get it out of us. So we knew that any extra cash we gave Richie would find it's way to her. If only we thought she would have used it to care for the children. Ultimately, Lucas left him enough cash for two meals a day. Richie ended up eating one meal a day and spending the remaining money on cigarettes and a calling card to call Endora.

Chapter Eleven

Richie also used his calling card to give us regular updates on how the training was going and how the kids were faring. The reports were not encouraging. We also heard from other family members that when they called Endora or stopped by the house, she would not let them in or allow contact with the kids. We didn't even try, knowing Endora was angry with us for taking Richie in. She had told him that the utilities were about to be cut off, and the phone indeed was. Endora just went out and got a cell phone, with what money, I have no idea. At this point Lucas and I started to have real concerns that those kids' lives might be in jeopardy. At the very least, they would not have a Christmas that year. When I thought about how excited Fancy Free had been on the previous Christmas Eve when Lucas had come out dressed as Santa, I felt sick. She had been so shocked to see Santa that she just shook from head to toe. This year she might not even get any Christmas dinner.

On Christmas Eve morning, Lucas and I and our youngest daughter, Julia, drove over with gifts for the kids. It was so cold I didn't want to get out of the car, but we knocked on the front door. After a long delay, Endora opened the door a few inches; just enough for us to see that she was dressed only from the waist up. She managed to stick her bare leg into the small opening she had created so that we couldn't see inside at all. I stood on Endora's front porch and thought *the woman was crazy.* When we showed her our gifts for the kids, she pushed Fancy Free out the door onto the front porch and shut it behind her. The child had on a tee shirt and no shoes. Lucas immediately took off his coat and threw it around her, then lifted her onto his knee so that her bare feet weren't touching the freezing concrete. She looked horrible. Her black curly hair probably hadn't been combed in weeks. Her tee shirt was filthy. Her eyes had big dark rings under them. We could think of nothing to say that wouldn't hurt her, so she took the gift silently, gave each of us a big hug, and then turned back into the house. We heard Joel crying as the door closed behind her, and then heard him getting even more upset because his sister had a present and he didn't. The door opened again, just enough to push Joel out, and then closed. Joel was very unsure of us; we hadn't seen him for a while, and he was only two. We handed him his gift and told him we loved him. He took it and turned back to the door, which opened just long enough to let him back in. Joel had looked as bad as his sister, like cast members from a production of *Oliver.* It was the most horrifying experience of my life. We drove home thinking, *what should we do?*

It was December 26, 2001, the day after Christmas. I knew something had to be done, I just wasn't sure what. Then I remembered that my friend Stewart, whose daughter I coached in softball, was a social worker. I wasn't sure what his specific job was, but figured it was worth a try. It turned out that he worked for the Division of Family Services in the city. I described the situation, and he said that as a caseworker, he would love to help me, but unfortunately Endora lived out of his jurisdiction. The area of Missouri that we live in is big enough that DFS has separated jurisdiction by city and county lines. He did go on to explain how I could hotline Endora to the county DFS jurisdiction. Then they would have to go check on the kids. He gave me the number and told me to call him back if I ran into any problems. So I called DFS and explained that no one had seen the kids for weeks before Christmas Eve and that they looked really bad. I expressed our concern regarding Endora's lack of money, the utilities apparently having been turned off, and her history of unstable behavior. Given the fact that her husband had left her with two young children and no money, her emotional state could only have worsened. The response from the woman on the other end of the line was, "Ma'am, have you actually been in the house?" I had to tell her "no." That was exactly why I was concerned. She said, "If you haven't been in the house and actually seen that things are bad, then we can't waste our time coming out to check on the children." Wow! So sorry to have bothered her!

I immediately called Stewart back. He was livid and apologetic. After we talked for a while, he said that he would talk with his supervisor to see if there was some way that he could help us. Later, he told me that his supervisor had told him only what he already knew, that they had no jurisdiction because he worked for the city not the county.

He did have an off-the-record suggestion: Stewart could stop by and flash his badge. If Endora didn't look at it closely, she might let him in. If so, Stewart would be able to see that conditions were bad and hotline the case to the county, having actually been in the house. We planned his visit for December 28th.

Endora happened to live very close to a restaurant at which I was meeting the softball team that evening for our team Christmas party. Stewart and I would see each other there, and he would have stopped by Endora's house and be able to tell me how bad the situation was there.

When I saw Stewart walk through the door of the restaurant I knew it wasn't good. We'd arrived before the girls so that we could talk. His first words were, "Rene, I would put the living conditions in that house on my top-ten list of the worst I have ever seen." Working in the city, he had seen some bad stuff. At Endora's house, he saw boxes of junk stacked from floor to ceiling in every room, leaving no paths to walk through. Everything was filthy; nothing had been cleaned for at least six months. Dirty clothes, dirty dishes, and trash everywhere. There was fecal matter smeared on every wall, and burn marks all over the kitchen ceiling. Endora had decided that it was a good idea to light candles on top of the cabinets. Cigarette butts covered the tables, counters, and floors. Moldy food sat out everywhere, leading to in infestation of roaches. Worst part? Endora and the kids were missing.

When Stewart had first arrived, Endora's landlord was there. Stewart told him who he was and why he had come. The landlord said that he had just been inside the house and was just sick at what he saw. The only silver lining, was that there were two PODs sitting in the driveway, so he knew she was packing up to move. He and Stewart walked through the house together. The guy was so angry at the damage that had been done to his property that Stewart thought he was going to blow up. It was a home that a normal mind could never conceive of living in by choice. Stewart went out to his car and hot lined the county. Then he came over to the restaurant to let me know what he had discovered. After talking with me he left to go back to the house to meet up with a county caseworker that was coming out to see things.

While Stewart was at the restaurant telling me all of this, Endora and kids showed back up at the house. The landlord was angry enough to tear Endora's hair out, but since he couldn't do anything physical to her he let the anger flow from his lips, telling her that she was finally going to get what she deserved, since DFS had just been there and were on their way back. While he was still yelling, Endora hopped in the car and took off.

If only that landlord had kept his mouth shut, this whole story might have turned out differently. Endora and the kids would have gone into the house, and when DFS showed up they could have and probably would have taken immediate custody of Joel and Fancy Free. But because of that one mistake, that one outburst of emotion, for which I don't blame him, we lost the best chance we would ever have to protect those kids.

Endora knew from her experience as a doctor that all she had to do was remove the kids from the negative environment, and DFS could not take them. So she fled and never returned. The PODS Stewart had seen in the driveway told us that she was in the process of leaving for good anyway. We didn't know where she planned to go, but we suspected she was leaving town and going back to her home state of Alabama.

Now Endora was on the run and enraged. She called Richie and threatened him, thinking he was the one who turned her in to DFS. Richie must have reminded her that she couldn't leave the state of Missouri because she was still on probation and suggested to her to contact DFS. Since Stewart had left his business card with the landlord, who in turn gave it to Endora, she contacted him. She had been frightened enough by Stewart to contact him every time she moved to a new hotel. We never did let Richie know that Stewart was our friend. Even though he acted as though the kids were his life and everything he was now doing would help them in the future, we were skeptical. After all, he had left the children in Endora's care to begin with.

Through records of phone conversations with Richie and Stewart, we were able to find out where Endora was staying. I gave the information to Stewart so that he could check up on the kids. He showed up at the hotel room door and flashed his badge. He managed to put the fear of God in her and made her believe that every time she moved she would be required to contact him so that he could check on the kids. This, of course, was untrue; Stewart still had no jurisdiction over her. But she fell for it.

Now in a state of paranoia, Endora never returned to

the house to retrieve her belongings. The facility where she and Richie had put everything in storage began calling Lucas. They hadn't received a payment in months. We knew that everything there, was Endora's and it had been a joke to bring it to town to begin with, since she had no use or room for it. We never did send the storage facility any more money, so it's pretty safe to assume the owners confiscated everything. Here is an educated couple and they are completely out of money. They have a house and storage facility filled with items they will never use again and it never occurs to either one of them to just start selling the stuff. This would have generated some money for food and utilities, if nothing else. But in the end they just walked away from all of it including: birth certificates, medical records, pictures, and keepsakes from Endora's whole life.

Chapter Twelve

Richie returned to our home the first week in January, having successfully completed truck-driver training and needing to find a job. Meanwhile, after Stewart met Endora and the kids he had called and asked if Lucas and I would consider taking in both children. He didn't have any authority over the situation, but felt the children should be removed from Endora's care. She was jumping from hotel to hotel about every three days at that point. If she were to go into the city , and Stewart could keep her there long enough, then there was a chance he could move in and take the kids from her. He was calling us in preparation.

I was honest and told him I just didn't see any way I could raise a four-year old and a two-year old and keep the commitments I had made to my own children. For example, Julia's softball team, which I coached, would play at least sixty games from April through July, and I also had to attend close to ninety games of Nikki's that same summer. The thought of trying to pull this off without one of Endora's kids getting hurt was just too much. I wouldn't be able keep an eye on them all of the time, so it was too dangerous to bring them to games. Stewart completely understood, as he lived in this same world. One of his daughters played for me and he coached another, just like I did. We spent every weekend at the ballpark, usually on Friday night and then from sunup until sundown both Saturday and Sunday. Also, there were league games one night a week. Four days a week, not counting a practice night. But I explained to Stewart that I had been talking with Neal and Maria, and that they were considering taking one of the kids. We would alternate weekends so the kids could spend them together. On weekends we had the kids, Lucas would help me with them and the team, and we would pull it off together. Stewart explained up front that DFS would rather see the kids stay together, but that our solution would be better than placing them with foster parents outside of the family.

Lucas and I contacted Maria and told her the time had come for them to decide if they were really ready to make this commitment. Maria and Neal spent that evening talking with their children about taking in Joel. Only one of their three boys still lived at home, and he was nineteen, but they still felt it had to be a family decision; they would need help from time to time from the boys. We knew what they were wrestling with; we all understood that Endora was not going to get better overnight. In fact, she would probably never be a fit mother. So Joel and Fancy Free would be permanent additions to our families. If the decision were made to take these kids in, we wanted them to know that they would always have a home with us. In other words, we were all willing to adopt them. We had the same conversation with our girls about Fancy Free. They needed to understand that there would be babysitting duties, their stuff would get broken, they would lose some privacy, and a host of other changes would occur.

The next morning, Maria called me and said that they had decided, as a family, to step in and help. Maria and I felt that they should take Joel, as they had raised three boys and felt more at ease with him, and we were raising three girls so we could handle Fancy Free a little better. We had been around the situation long enough to realize that they were going to have issues we had never had to address in raising our own children. Maria and I felt that we would each be able to identify a potential problem sooner if they were raising a boy and we were raising a girl. We would know right away whether a certain behavior was normal or out of the ordinary without having to adjust to the difference between little boys and little girls.

I contacted Stewart and suggested that we all have lunch that Saturday so that he could meet Neal and Maria. At lunch, Stewart told us that this would not be a slam-dunk, since family courts always give the mother chance after chance to screw up again and again. We told him we felt there was a way to get Joel out, but that DFS would have to step in to help Fancy Free. Richie wasn't her biological father, and we had no way of finding that man. We had not even talked with Richie about any of this. He had been away from Endora and the kids for more than four weeks, and during that time had never indicated that he was considering asking for custody. We knew he thought that if he got a job and was sending support to Endora, he would have done all he could do for his son and step-daughter. After talking with Stewart for several hours, the four of us decided to sit down with Richie and see where he stood.

Chapter Thirteen

I remember that afternoon so vividly. Richie was living in our finished basement, and spent most of his time down there either on the computer or watching TV. Maria and I and our husbands drove straight from our lunch with Stewart to our house, and headed to the basement to have a chat with Richie. Richie's arrogance and pride required that it be handled delicately. If we insulted him in any way or seemed to be trying to control him we would get nowhere. But we had to be firm. The men did most of the talking while Maria and I listened. They explained our concern for the welfare of both of the kids, and that it had nothing to with whether we liked or disliked Endora. Much to my surprise, Richie agreed but felt that his hands were tied. He knew that he could get Joel out, but he also knew he had no claim to Fancy Free, and feared what taking Joel away would do to his sister. All that five-year old girl had in the world was her three-year old brother. Her emotional health depended on him; she had no parent to care for her or give her attention. Of course, Richie may have told himself this to avoid the responsibility of having to care for Joel.

It took a lot of persuasion, but we finally got Richie to understand our position. We loved Fancy Free as much as

Joel and would do everything we could to help her if the courts would allow it. If they wouldn't, that was no reason to let Joel go down with a ship that was definitely sinking. I know it sounds callous to talk of leaving a child behind. But the other option was to leave them both behind. Richie planned to find an attorney on Monday.

Several days after our discussion, Richie had an appointment with an attorney to discuss custody of the kids, as well as a divorce; something he now seemed to want. Endora had continued to call our house, harass Richie, and accuse him of causing every problem in her life. She had his car, and he offered several times to take the kids so that she could begin a serious hunt for a job. She refused, as she was too paranoid to give up control of the kids. She had already lost control of Richie, and was rapidly losing control of herself. It was apparent that she had stopped taking medication.

That morning, Lucas and Richie prepared for the meeting. (Lucas was to attend, since he was paying the bill.) Richie revealed to Lucas that he and Endora had filed no tax returns since 1998, a new piece of information that just about sent Lucas over the edge. I've seen him pretty upset, but never like that. His brother, an ex–military man, ex–prosecuting attorney, had not paid any taxes for three or four years. All I could think to do was call Neal and Maria. Neal has always been like a big brother to Lucas, and might have been the only person able to keep him from hurting his own brother.

Maria and Neal both left work immediately. They met at home, packed for a few nights, and began the two-hour drive to town. Neal called Lucas several times from the road to try to keep him calm. When they got to our house, the guys decided that they would both accompany Richie to the meeting at the attorney's office. Maria and I decided to try to meet up with Endora. Perhaps if we could convince her that we wanted to help, we could avoid getting the courts or the child welfare system involved. And if we could get the kids away from her, it was a safe bet she'd get herself into trouble pretty quickly, making a custody suit easier. We got a hold of her at the phone number that had been showing up on our caller ID, and she actually agreed to meet with us at 4:00 that afternoon.

Endora was now staying at a place called Studio Suites, in another part of town, part of the county. It was the type of place where corporations put up employees when they are in town for an extended period of time. Not just a hotel room, but also a suite with a small kitchen and living room. Of course, the first thing we thought was, *how is she paying for this?* A question that had been on our minds the whole time she was on the run: nineteen days now. How was she paying for all those hotel rooms? I still can't answer that question, but there's no doubt it was illegal. She had no money. None.

When we got to Studio Suites, Endora was not there. We called her cell phone; she was up the street at Walgreen's. She told us to stay there and she'd come right back. When she pulled into the parking lot, Maria and I went over to help her. She had several bags and the kids were out of the car and running in the parking lot before Endora even got her door open. They ran to us immediately, looking healthy but unkempt. As we grabbed Endora's bags we got a look at the inside of the car. No words can accurately describe its condition. Richie had already told us that the car was unlicensed and uninsured. It was a 1989 model, faded gray with the usual amount of body damage one would expect in a car that old. The tires were bad, and as we looked we wondered what else might be ready to go; like the brakes. It didn't take a rocket scientist to figure out that if the car wasn't licensed, it probably hadn't been inspected for over a year. The kids' lives could have been in jeopardy every time they rode in it.

Issues relating to the car would come up repeatedly in the future. Endora got pulled over numerous times for having expired license plates. Each time the kids were in the car with her. It was always filthy, Endora always looked and acted out of sorts, and the car was uninsured. Yet not one police officer ever thought of checking with DFS to see if there was an open case involving this family, or a father who could care for the children. The problem was just too small for them, not important enough. The law says we have to have our cars inspected once a year for the purpose of keeping us safe. The citations Endora received didn't accomplish that.

Once we took everything out of the car and had the kids under control so they weren't darting all over the parking lot, we headed up to their room. It was not clean, but was sort of picked up. We immediately noticed a black burn mark on the wall around the electrical socket, but didn't want to start things off on the wrong foot by asking about it. Fancy Free told us days later that Joel had stuck something into the socket and the wall had caught on fire. She didn't say where Endora had been at the time.

Endora began to unpack her purchases, including some grocery items and toys for the kids. She had bought them blow pens and clay to play with. She had been ranting and mumbling to herself since getting out of the car, and she looked worse than usual. That was saying a lot. With her heavy eye makeup and the way her hair hung, she always looked rough around the edges. Sometimes she seemed to know we were there; other times we weren't so sure. She spent our first hour in the room going off on Richie. We chose not to say anything, just let her vent. One minute she was raging mad and the next crying. From a woman's point of view, we could understand such emotion; after all, her husband had left her with two small children and no money. But the logical part of our brains, something Endora seemed to lack, reminded us that she had been offered help several times. She knew that Richie had no money to give her, and that we would watch the kids anytime she wanted to search for a job or a place to live. She never let anyone help her, so our empathy for her emotional stress had limits. Most of it could have been avoided.

We couldn't always follow her speech. That day I realized just how mentally ill she actually was. I'd never been around someone with such severe emotional problems. Sometimes she sounded fairly lucid, but at other times it was like being in a room full of rubber balls bouncing off the walls and ceiling. Where do you look; what should you focus on?

Endora paid no attention to her children, even when we called something to her attention. She couldn't focus long enough to care. As we entered the room, I noticed that Joel had something in his mouth. I said, "Endora, I think Joel has something in his mouth. I'm worried he could choke." She looked at him as if she would do something about it, but a moment later it was as if it had never been mentioned. After making the point another time and getting the same kind of response, Maria stuck a finger in his mouth and pulled out eight plastic game pieces. Later, as Maria was trying to get through to Endora, I noticed that Joel was taking apart the toilet. It was kind of funny to see the little guy disappear into the bathroom and emerge each time with another piece. First the lid, then some bolts. He even managed to remove the ball from the tank. I said, "Endora, I'm going to help Joel. He's having some issues with the toilet," but she forgot about it even before her head turned fully around to look at him.

The kids had started complaining about hunger as soon as we walked into the room. Endora put some frozen White Castle burgers into the microwave. An hour later, when the kids started crying again for something to eat, she remembered the burgers.

After the kids ate, they wanted to play with their new stuff, so out came the blow pens. They terrorized the room with them. Within twenty minutes ink from the markers covered their faces and hands, the carpet and blankets; by morning when we returned, it had reached the TV and the walls. Once they tired of the markers, they broke out the clay, making an unbelievable mess right under Endora's nose. Busy talking about her life, Richie, her career, her feelings, and her situation, she took no notice of the kids. She never even mentioned them.

Endora settled down enough after that first hour that we felt comfortable offering up suggestions to her, representing ourselves as two women wanting to help another woman in a very stressful situation. We told her that we would be feeling the same way if our husbands had left us under those circumstances. We prioritized the things she would need to do to care for the children and herself. First, get a job. How, when she had the two kids, she asked. What would she do with them when called for an interview? We offered to help. She claimed to have a job interview at the police station at 10:00 the following morning. Classic Endora, we hadn't gotten her settled down for more than ten minutes, and she was already lying to us. A dispatching job with the police, with her arrest record, probation, and pending charges for shoplifting and invalid license plates? But we played along.

After much hesitation, she agreed to let us watch the kids while she went on the "interview." We could tell she was afraid to leave the kids with us, fearing we would run off with them. Ironic, since she was the one running. Maria and I agreed to return at 9:00 a.m. to watch the kids until Endora returned. She made it clear that we must stay in the room. We still believed the job interview was a fabrication, but played along and made the plans. It seemed that Endora believed her own lie.

We tried to guide the conversation back toward prioritizing. Since it was unlikely she would get hired on the spot, even if they did like her for the "job," she needed to get other things accomplished that would be difficult with the kids around. Like using the computer at the library to get her resume in order, so she could apply for other jobs. Once she got one, she could look for a permanent place to live, and work on finding adequate childcare. We cautiously suggested that if she let the kids stay with us for a while, she would have a better chance of accomplishing all this. Maria offered to take Joel to her house, and I did the same for Fancy Free. We made clear that the kids would be together on the weekends, and she would be able to call or visit them at any reasonable time of the day or evening. We did ask that she be willing to work with us on the last part, as we had kids too and might not always be available. She was not happy about the kids being separated, but acted as if it was a reasonable compromise. It was agreed that the next morning she would go on her interview and we would watch the children in the suite. After she returned, Maria and I would leave with the kids. Endora had admitted to us during the discussion that DFS had been on her back, and believed that if she completed the tasks we laid out it would help her situation with them. We could not have agreed more enthusiastically.

Since this entire scenario was to begin with a job interview we knew did not exist, it was sure to be interesting.

Chapter Fourteen

Maria and I returned to Studio Plus the following morning at 9:00 and knocked on the door. No answer. We returned to the lobby and called the room. Endora answered on the seventh ring, with a hoarse, just-woken-up voice. She was not going to let us in, nor was she going to her interview. No surprise there. She had returned to trusting no one.

The previous evening, Richie had angered us by going to see Endora after we had left. They always fought, so we feared the meeting could lead only to more conflict. We were right. For not the first and not the last time, Richie had undone the progress we had made. Endora did say that she would talk with us later, so we hung out in the lobby.

At noon, she still wasn't answering the phone and the employees at the Studio Suites had started to shoot us inquisitive stares. One of them got up the nerve to strike up a conversation, giving us the opportunity to explain the situation and ask whether they had noticed any unusual behavior. Indeed, they had witnessed the kids running up and down the halls and playing in the stairwells unsupervised, stairwells with no handrails to prevent the kids from falling over. One of the employees decided to help us by knocking on the door and telling Endora that management needed to look at the carpet, as they were planning to replace it. That was actually true, so if Endora didn't answer, she planned to use the passkey. A few minutes later the woman returned and informed us with a smile that everyone was now awake. We thanked her and headed straight for the room.

As soon as we got there, Fancy Free told us that she and Joel both had their own grocery sacks packed with belongings. "Rene, I'm coming home with you and Joel is going to Maria's." But though Endora had promised her children that this would happen and could see the excitement in their faces, she thought nothing of changing her mind.

Endora was angry with Richie after his behavior the night before. He had informed her of his meeting with the attorney, and his petitions for divorce and for custody of Joel. Since she was doing nothing to better her life or the lives of the children, she would be served with a petition for an Order of Protection for Joel, meaning Richie would be trying to get immediate custody of Joel to protect his well-being. I'm sure none of this made any sense to her, since it contradicted the arrangement she and Maria and I had just spent four hours coming up with. Now, we all knew that it was necessary for Richie to take those legal actions; but Richie getting in her face to show her that he had one-upped her succeeded only in angering her again. We could never trust Endora to comply with anything she promised to do. However, if Richie had been as concerned for the kids as we were, he would have kept his mouth shut and the kids would have already been with us by the time Endora was served with papers.

Any trust we gained from her the night before had vanished. The deal was off, and she planned to leave for Alabama that day with the kids. They began to cry.

It took about an hour to calm Endora down. The room was in shambles, so we asked her if we could dress the kids and take them to lunch so that she could clean up. In addition to the papers, stencils, pens, and clay that had been there the night before, we now saw food, cigarettes (smoked and unsmoked), and tampons lying all over the floor. The place reeked of cigarette smoke, poison to the asthmatic Joel.

At McDonald's, the kids were excited to come live with us, but we tried to ease them into the idea that their mom might have changed her mind. When we returned from lunch with the kids, the door was unlocked. We knocked and were told to come in. The door opened to reveal a haze of smoke from the waist up as thick as fog. I couldn't believe one person could create so much smoke. The room had been picked up, and it didn't take long to find out why. Endora had talked with her probation officer about leaving the state. The officer told her that she could not leave without violating her probation. The question had apparently aroused suspicion, since the officer insisted on coming over to visit sometime that day.

Maria and I were praying that since we had brought the kids back, just like we said we would, a window of trust might open in Endora again. She told us that she was concerned about what the probation officer was going to do with her. She and the kids had to be out of the Studio Suites by 11:00 a.m. the next day. Endora was down to her last three hundred dollars. If she did not let the kids come with us they would all be homeless. We wondered where the three hundred dollars had come from in the first place, but we never did ask. After much discussion she agreed, once again, to let us have the kids. She asked us to come back the next morning at 10:00 a.m., when she would give us the kids and begin life on her own. When we got home, Richie said, "She's just playing you."

Chapter Fifteen

When we arrived at the Studio Suites the next morning, January 18, 2002, the front desk informed us that Endora and the kids had left at 8:30 that morning. We called Richie, who called Endora's probation officer, fearing she had left the state with his son. The probation officer told us that Endora was due in her office at 11:00 a.m. sharp. If she were even five minutes late they would issue a warrant for her arrest. In the meantime, Lucas and Richie had appeared in court and Richie was granted an Order of Protection, giving him temporary custody of Joel.

Maria and I left the Studio Suites and headed to the Federal Building in the City, where the probation office was located and where we were to meet our husbands and Richie. We hoped Endora would make her appointment, and we would get Joel. The court could do nothing to protect Fancy Free, since she was not Richie's child.

When Endora showed up, she and Richie and the kids were shuffled into a room with the probation officer while the rest of us waited in the cafeteria. Once Richie produced the custody papers, Joel was allowed to go with him. Richie gave him to Neal and Maria, who immediately left for home with Joel.

At certain points in this story, it becomes clear that

some people in the child welfare system do their jobs because they like them and because society needs them, but to others, it's just a job and the favored resolution is always the easiest one. Endora's probation officer knew her history. With a little checking, they would have known that Endora had been cited many times for vehicle violations in recent weeks and, though we did not know it at the time, they would have found outstanding arrest warrants for passing bad checks. They also knew that when she left the building she would be homeless and she and Fancy Free would have to live either in her car or in a shelter. To top it off, they were aware that her late model car was unlicensed, uninsured, and not inspected. Richie had informed them that the tires were ready to blow.

And then, of course, there was the fact that anyone in a room with Endora for more than five minutes could tell she was unstable and in no condition to take care of herself, much less a child. With Joel having been taken away, she was in a total frenzy. An unlicensed car was a minor infraction, but the endangerment of a child was not. We thought the probation officer would have enough sense to use that minor infraction to call in DFS to protect Fancy Free. Here was a family waiting to take care of her, and Fancy Free pleading for Richie to take her, too. But we watched Endora walk out of the building with her little girl. When the probation officer emerged, we confronted her about Fancy Free and got nothing more than a shrug of her shoulders and an "It's not my problem."

That night the phone calls from Endora began. She wanted Neal and Maria's phone number and she was threatening to kill Richie and Lucas. She persisted in leaving messages for several hours. Finally I had had enough and answered the phone. I told her it was time to grow up. She seemed taken aback, so I went on to remind her that she had reneged on the deal she had made with Maria and me. She was now seeing the result of her choice. Had she let Maria and I take in the kids, she would be able to talk with both of them. Now that she was calling our house and harassing our family, there was no way we were giving her Neal and Maria's number so she could do the same to them.

Chapter Sixteen

From January until the beginning of March 2002, Endora would live in four different locations that we knew of within and around town. She was hopping from place to place with Fancy Free in tow, and how she paid for it was anyone's guess.

When Richie appeared in court on January 18, Joel was assigned a guardian Ad Litem (GAL), an attorney who was to represent Joel's best interests, to be his voice and to make decisions that were good for him. Richie's attorney explained to us that she was not meant to be concerned with the emotional state of Richie or Endora, only with protecting Joel. In theory, this was a good plan, but we would soon learn that there were too many children like Joel and not enough guardians to go around. Guardians were assigned more cases than they could handle, so they breezed over each one without having time to properly research or investigate. They listened to what each parent had to say, and if DFS was involved, listened to their opinion. Then they made a recommendation to the judge as to who should have custody of the child. The judge, who had even less time to get involved in the details, almost always followed the guardian's recommendation.

Richie's attorney knew which GAL was going to be

assigned to Joel before the appearance in court: Gale Shoffler. So Richie made an appointment to meet with her. Lucas was busy so I went along as none of us trusted Richie to do anything for the children on his own.

Ms. Shoffler was all business, as expected. With her caseload she had no time for chitchat. Afterward, Richie felt he had bonded quite well with her, since she, too, was retired from the armed forces. I wasn't so sure. After all, she was a woman, and Richie had now left two families. I listened to Richie's version of the story as he told it to Ms. Shoffler, all the while observing her reactions. She kept a good poker face but I could tell she had questions about why Richie had conducted himself the way he had, especially his decision to have another child with Endora.

The truth was, I went along with Richie to the meeting to make exactly that point. I wanted her to know that none of us felt Richie was a fit parent, either, and that the Howitt family was not simply ganging up on Endora. The difference was this: if she recommended awarding custody of Joel to Richie, he had family that would help. Unlike Endora, Richie admitted that he was incapable of caring for the children, ostensibly because of his job as a truck driver. I also wanted to let the GAL know that if she could do anything to help Fancy Free, our family would be there for her as well. Ms. Shoffler was informed at this meeting that if Richie gained custody of Joel, he would turn him over to his sister Maria. She learned from this conversation who really cared about the kids, not their parents, and that we wanted to help Fancy Free just as much as Joel. She knew the four of us would be in it for the duration.

Even more important, I made it clear that we were more disappointed in Richie than we were in Endora, since we expected Richie to know better. He had been raised in a family with strong values. At least Endora had an excuse; her childhood mirrored that of her kids. That was all Ms. Shoffler knew. She told the judge to grant Richie custody.

So now Joel lived with Neal and Maria, and had the kind of life he and his sister had only dreamed of. Fancy Free, unfortunately, was worse off than ever, as Endora's anger was at a peak, and she couldn't afford her medication. They jumped from place to place, staying up all night and sleeping all day, living in filthy, confined motel rooms. Endora chain-smoked, paced, raged. Fancy Free lived on junk food and soda, which she got only when she cried for it. She witnessed every raging phone call and every face-to-face fight between her mother and Richie during Richie's frequent visits, which probably also included sex. She saw her mother crying one minute, a foul-mouthed dragon the next. How do I know all this? We heard it on the other end of the phone line.

While Neal and Maria tried their best to take care of Joel, Endora did everything she could to interfere. They both worked full time and needed to put Joel into some type of daycare. To do that, they needed his medical records to be sure he had received the proper immunizations. Richie couldn't remember the name of his pediatrician, and Endora refused to give it to us. Any records that Endora had kept on her children had been shoveled into a POD container with the rest of the mess she'd left at their house. What the landlord did with the filth he shoveled out: hauled it to a dump, burned it, we never knew. After he had completed this task he wiped his hands of anyone named Howitt and refused to answer our questions.

We knew that Fancy Free had briefly attended pre-school, so we started our search there. They were able to give us the name of the last pediatrician they had on record, but that doctor had since died. So we were forced to go back to Endora and beg for the information. She was a doctor, but she just didn't get it. We told her that daycare was not optional, neither Neal nor Maria were going to quit their jobs so either she gave us the information or her son would have to get all of his immunization shots again. She told us nothing.

During my many phone conversations with Endora, when she called to ask us to take Fancy Free to see Joel, she revealed that she had been talking to her sister, Clara, and her best friend, Diane. Clara lived in Kentucky; Diane lived in Georgia. According to Richie, neither of their husbands could stand Endora, and both refused to have anything to do with her. But both women remained loyal, which may explain where Endora had been getting some of her money.

Endora told me that Fancy Free was going to stay with Diane for a couple of weeks while Endora searched for a job and a permanent place to live. Of course, this was exactly what Maria and I had offered to do. We were happy that Diane was willing to help, but did she know what she was getting into? Her husband also needed to know, since the situation was not going to resolve itself in only a couple of weeks. We felt it was only fair to fill them in.

We contacted Diane. I wanted Diane to know that it was kind of her to take in Fancy Free, but that Fancy Free would be unable to see her brother often if she went to Georgia. Endora knew this, but as usual, the most important thing to her was that she controlled the situation. Diane also needed to understand that this was a long-term commitment; the chances of Endora getting a job that paid enough to support her kids were very slim. Endora's condition had regressed so much that she would never be able to get through an interview, let alone a day on the job. Richie had suggested to us that Diane's husband might not be happy about the situation, and if that was the case, she needed to consider what it could do to their relationship. Most important, if she and her husband could not be in it for the long haul, their getting involved at all would not be fair to Fancy Free.

We had also stayed in contact with Endora's sister after Joel went home with Maria, wanting her to know how bad the situation was here. She needed to understand how very sick her sister was, and that losing Joel was going to make her worse. Clara seemed to understand and even told us she believed our version of the story; Endora's parenting reminded Clara of her own mother, Iris. When I told her that Fancy Free was surviving on candy and soda, she said that was exactly what they had gotten for breakfast every morning. Endora had called her for help, but Clara's husband would not let her get involved. Clara may have been helping Endora behind her husband's back;

after all, Endora was her sister. But I tried to make her see that every time she sent Endora money, she was prolonging Fancy Free's hell. As long as Endora could survive that way, she would. Also, Neal and Maria wanted Clara to know that our purpose was not to take Joel away from his family; they would frequently e-mail her pictures and updates on her nephew.

I invited both Clara and Diane to come to town and stay with us, so that they could witness firsthand what was going on. Then they could form their own opinions of the situation; there could be no question whose version of the story was more accurate. If they thought we were wrong, we would accept that. But if they saw what we saw, their opinions would carry more weight with Endora, and certainly with a judge, than ours would. Endora had always successfully sold the story that the big, bad Howitts were ganging up on poor little her. But neither Clara nor Diane ever came to Missouri.

My friend Stewart maintained contact with Endora and Fancy Free for a while. Endora never knew that he had no jurisdiction over her, or that he was my friend, so he was able to inspire fear in her. On January 22, he called to let me know that he thought he might have worked out an agreement with her. She told Stewart that she was willing to let Fancy Free stay with us until the following conditions had been met: getting a job and keeping it for three consecutive months; finding a decent, safe place to live; beginning to see a psychiatrist at least once a month; and remaining on her medication. For our part, we would agree to let Endora visit with both of the kids, and make sure the kids saw each other often. Stewart said that Endora was willing to put this in writing. I told him that we believed it still needed to be decided in a court of law, and that we would still need to meet with Endora. Some very important issues had yet to be addressed: she needed to have affordable childcare in place, attend some parenting classes, and maintain a cleaner home; not that we ever believed these things would occur. Stewart agreed that making it legal was a very good idea, but predicted that Endora would never be able to keep a job for three consecutive months. We didn't know then just how right he was.

When Stewart brought up the idea of making the agreement legal, Endora immediately reneged and that was the end of that. It was just another of her games. At that point, Stewart contacted the county DFS to let them know where Endora was staying, how often she was jumping around, and what he had witnessed. He suggested that they stay on top of the case because Fancy Free was in danger. One would think that any professional in the field would have appreciated the legwork that Stewart had already done for them. But the county caseworker assigned to the case took issue with Stewart calling him. No one was going to tell him how to do his job. We never saw any respect or cooperation between caseworkers in different offices, only turf wars: as a rule, different jurisdictions of DFS, whether within a state or across state lines, do not share information they have obtained on a family. Endora would soon find this out and use this flaw in the system to her advantage.

Until Endora finally landed an apartment in the beginning of March, we did our best to keep up with her. Neal and Maria wanted to let Joel have contact with her by phone; though the three-year old had begun to call Maria "Mommy" from the moment they brought him home, and therefore needed the name and number of Endora's latest motel. Not wanting her to have their phone number, they wouldn't call her cell phone. Endora knew that if she wanted to talk with Joel, all she had to do was call us. We would contact Neal and Maria immediately, and they would call her at whatever motel she was staying at. They had agreed to let Endora visit Joel, but when they informed her that each visit had to be approved by Gale Shoffler, she became belligerent. We also wanted DFS to check in on Fancy Free as often as possible. The county was obligated to look into the situation, but not to listen to Stewart any further, which they didn't. And Endora wanted no authority figure telling her what to do, so she refused to tell us where she was staying. Her cell phone service had been shut off, so she began to call our house from different Kinko's locations. Her calls always came in the evening; she and Fancy Free never got out of bed before the late afternoon.

Richie's attorney attempted to find Endora, since she needed to be served papers regarding their upcoming court date for a custody hearing. She knew this, but was trying to avoid going to court even though it was the only way to get her son back.

Chapter Seventeen

February 7, 2002, was the second court date, the first had been when Richie got the Order of Protection for Joel, but it was the first time we all appeared at the same time. Endora had finally been served with papers, and we were told she had an attorney. Neal, Maria, Lucas, and I had been looking forward to the date for weeks, believing we would finally have a chance to talk to a judge about Fancy Free. We would end the day disappointed and disillusioned.

Endora had successfully avoided being served since January, but her attorney and Gale Shoffler informed her that if she wanted any chance at getting Joel back she would ultimately have to appear. So she finally let them track her down.

Neal and Maria came into town with Joel the night before the hearing. Richie got to spend some time with him, and even though Joel enjoyed seeing his father, we could see the confusion in his eyes. The next morning the five of us arrived at the courthouse by 9:00 a.m. As usual, we left Joel with one of our girls, and asked a neighbor to keep an eye out in case Endora decided to leave the courthouse and attempt to kidnap her son.

Endora and Fancy Free sat there with her attorney on

a wooden bench in the hallway outside the courtrooms. We sat across and down the hall from them, but we could all see each other. Fancy Free didn't look good. She looked at us and obviously wanted to come over, but knew this would be a betrayal of her mother. Soon Endora became engrossed in a conversation with her attorney, Lucas and Neal were busy discussing the situation with Richie and his attorney. Fancy Free gradually began to slide down the bench toward Maria and me. So we moved across the hall to the bench on the same side as her. The closer she got to us the more her smile widened. Still, it was easy to see the big brown circles under her eyes; she wasn't sleeping. When she finally made it all the way over, she gave us each a big hug and asked, "Where's Joel?"

Endora hadn't noticed her daughter move toward us, but Fancy Free slid back over to her and said, "See, Mommy? We're all friends." Endora told her not to come near us again. But when it came time to enter the courtroom, she left Fancy Free in the hall with us without a second thought.

Only Richie, Endora, their attorneys, and Gale Shoffler were allowed into the judge's chambers. Inside, Endora became very combative with the judge, telling her that she would be moving into the Bocker building soon, a place that provided childcare. She also told the judge that she had a job at a Jeep dealership and would be getting a Jeep to drive as a benefit. Based on those circumstances, she felt that Joel should be returned to her. The judge decided to postpone the hearing to give Gale Shoffler time to check out the new information. That made sense for Joel, who was in a safe place, but what about Fancy Free? Ms. Shoffler said her hands were tied; she had no legal grounds to bring Joel's sister up.

If Ms. Shoffler had taken the time to call DFS prior to the hearing, she would have known of their concerns about Fancy Free. On March 17, Richie received a letter from DFS stating that they "had found probable cause on both of the children." DFS had been out to Endora and Richie's old house back in December and had pictures of the living conditions, so why it took them that long to send the letter is anyone's guess. At the hearing on February 7 we did not have this letter in hand yet, but those pictures would have been available to enter as evidence. Perhaps they would have provided "legal grounds" to consider concerns regarding Fancy Free. If Gale Shoffler was too busy to contact DFS, could we count on her contacting the Bocker building and the Jeep dealership? We did it for her. The Bocker building did have condominium units up for sale, starting at an asking price of seventy thousand dollars. No way could Endora afford that, and there were no rental units in the building. We didn't need to check any further regarding childcare. There was no job with any Jeep dealership either; it was just another ruse to cover concerns about both her lack of employment and the vehicle she was driving. We left a message for Gale Shoffler saying that Endora had lied to the court.

Chapter Eighteen

It was eleven days after the hearing, and Endora had just played the hotel hop again. She called to say that she had gotten a new apartment and would be moving in within a couple of days. Richie had started a new job as an over-the-road truck driver, so anytime she wanted to talk with Richie she called us. He checked in with us every day to make sure Joel was okay and to get an update on Endora's activities. And he was still staying with us between truck runs. During my visits to pick up Fancy Free, I saw that Endora's new apartment was actually located in a decent neighborhood. It was a four-family brick building with arched doorways, high ceilings, and beautiful hardwood floors. Endora was no longer getting money from either Diane or Clara. She had no job. So she was either selling herself, selling drugs, or had developed the gift of con and gotten the manager to let her move in with no deposit. She may very well have been prostituting herself. But over the years it would become clear how easy it was for her to manipulate lawyers, judges, doctors, and hospital administrators, just to name a few, so it's not unbelievable that she got an apartment manager to believe whatever story she concocted.

At first she and Fancy Free slept on the floor, but after

a visit from DFS she was told that the children must have beds. The next day furniture showed up. She told us it was donated to her by a church.

Several weeks later we found out that the furniture was rented. Endora had paid for the rental and delivery with a bad check. She had rented a computer the same way. Once these vendors realized they had been taken, they looked up her last name in the phone book, and we got a call. This happened to us often. They all hoped that we would make good on her bad checks. We encouraged everyone who called to file a police report. It appeared to us that the only way we could help Fancy Free was to get Endora arrested. But the few reports that were filed moved through the system at a snail's pace.

Once Endora got the furniture, she decided that she needed to spruce up the place with paint, oil-based paint, that wouldn't wash off. She brought home some wild color and just slathered it on without covering the furniture or the floors. She didn't consider that she had ten-foot ceilings but no ladder, she just painted as high as she could reach. The beautiful floors and rented furniture were ruined.

Chapter Nineteen

At the end of February, once Endora had gotten settled in her new place, she seemed to want to work with us so that the kids could see each other. Though suspicious of her motives, we were excited to be able to spend time with Fancy Free. I had called Endora's new phone number to make sure that it was working, so that we could give it to Richie and stop being caught between them. During the conversation Endora told me that she would like the kids to see each other. I offered to pick Fancy Free up to spend the weekend with us and Neal and Maria. Endora asked me to call back the next evening at 6:30; she would have an answer for me then. So I followed her instructions, and got no answer. It was Friday night and I had places to drive my girls and their friends. I got home around 9:45 and Endora hadn't called, so I tried her again. She said I could pick Fancy Free up at 9:00 a.m. Saturday and have her until 5:00 p.m. Sunday.

Before driving all the way over, I called Endora; amazingly, she was still all right with the plan. So Lucas and I went over and picked up Fancy Free, and Endora gave us no trouble. We brought her home for a while so the girls could see her, and then took off for Neal and Maria's.

The visit ended up being very difficult on all of us.

Fancy Free could barely contain her excitement about seeing her brother during the two-hour drive there. But Joel was not so happy about seeing her. You can imagine his confusion: Fancy Free had been the only mother figure he had prior to Maria. The ability of a four or five-year old to take care of his needs were obviously going to fall way short of his experience living with Neal and Maria for the past month. His life had completely changed. Two adults now loved him as their own child. Three brothers played with him, took him to basketball games, and taught him to play football and baseball. He had his own room, and was expected to share in the responsibility of keeping it clean. He had a regular routine for bedtime and getting up, and got three good meals a day. If he behaved, he got the candy he had become addicted to, rationed, in a more balanced way instead of as his main course. He went to church and began to learn what life was really all about. Worship became a part of his everyday life, not just on Sunday mornings.

When he saw his sister approaching, he couldn't help but wonder if it was all coming to an end.

All Fancy Free knew was that her brother had been taken away, and she didn't understand why. His confusion and lack of compassion made her act aggressively, clinging to him and attempting to take charge. She started telling him what they were going to play and how, and he just looked at her, with no interest in playing. As the day progressed, Joel did open up and play with her, but Fancy Free was saddened to see that her brother lacked her excitement. Having never experienced anything resembling a normal home environment, she didn't understand Joel's attitude.

Neal and Maria had spent much of the last month teaching Joel to make decisions for himself. Not to be pushed around by others. He had lived with a dominating mother and sister his whole life, and was in danger of growing up into a wimp who would never be able to stand up to any woman in his life, much like his father. As they spent the day playing, we found ourselves frequently reminding him that they did not always have to do what Fancy Free wanted. This upset Fancy Free, she wasn't used to her brother contradicting her. During the ride home, we tried to help Fancy Free understand that she was Joel's sister, not his mother. That as equals, they must share in making decisions. We explained the upside: if Fancy Free were not always in charge, she would not always be held responsible when they got into trouble. Our attempts only made her angry, even after I moved to the back seat of the van with her. After a while I decided we should just spend time reading books, which she loved.

We had to take Julia to a softball game the next day, so Fancy Free spent that night at our house, sharing a bed with Nikki. We all attended the game, but since I coached the team, Lucas had to keep an eye on Fancy Free. He didn't have an easy time of it. In her five years, Fancy Free had rarely gone on a family outing and had never seen an organized sport played. She had no idea how to behave.

Though Fancy Free was a wonderful little girl and we loved her dearly, she already showed signs of extreme behavioral problems resulting from the life she had led with her mother. She remained loyal to Endora, but clearly would rather not have been living with her. I asked Fancy Free several times that weekend if she wanted to call her mom. The answer was always "no." Anytime we referred to it being time to go home, such as when we left Neal and Maria's house or the game, she wanted us to make it clear that we meant our home, not her mom's. Whenever she slept, she had bad dreams, her body trembling and jerking. She wet the bed, and even though we played it down, she insisted on blaming Nikki. Nikki, the most compassionate child I've ever known, just smiled.

At Julia's softball game, Fancy Free wanted to play with the other kids and became very angry with Lucas for trying to keep her close to him. She was not used to being watched or having restrictions of any kind. Most kids get upset when they are trying to play and their parents keep telling them to stay close, but Fancy Free's reactions were not normal. When Lucas picked her up to bring her back over to the area he was in, she screamed, "He's touching me, he's not my dad." She told Lucas she was going to spit in his face. We had raised three children and never seen anything like this.

Endora was so happy with how the weekend had gone, we actually returned Fancy Free as promised, and had given Endora some free time, that she soon called Maria to ask if she could see Joel herself. (Richie had caved in and given her Maria's number one night, so he could get off the phone and go back to sleep.) Neal and Maria agreed, but reminded her that it had to be approved through Ms. Shoffler. Endora became very angry at the idea of Ms.

Shoffler having to approve or even supervise her visit, and she took her anger out on Maria. Not knowing what to say, Maria let her vent. Then she reminded her that none of us had been allowed in the courtroom, so we had no way of knowing why this provision was in place. But since it was, Neal and Maria were required to get approval for Endora's visit. If they neglected to follow this procedure, all of them would be in trouble. Apparently Endora did not want to see Joel that badly, she never did call Ms. Shoffler to set it up, even though she called her on a regular basis to plead her case about regaining custody of Joel. Later we would find that she was winning this argument.

Chapter Twenty

On March 2, 2002, Maria and I and our husbands were to leave on a cruise we had been planning since the end of October. We were all pretty excited, never having been on a cruise ship. Joel would stay with Dan and Megan, Neal and Maria's son and daughter-in-law. All of this had been approved by DFS in the area where Neal and Maria lived, and also by Richie.

Fancy Free called that morning to ask if I would come over and take her for the weekend. I had to say no, explaining that I was going on a trip but would call her as soon as I got back. I didn't give her too much information, as we did not want Endora to know that all of us would be away. Fancy Free seemed to handle it pretty well. I told her that Lindsay, our oldest daughter, planned to come home from college to stay with her sisters, and Fancy Free could call her if she needed anything.

Unfortunately, child abuse doesn't take a vacation. So while the four of us were enjoying our weeklong cruise, our girls were left behind to deal with any problem that might arise for Fancy Free. They did the best they could, but their options were limited. They knew that even their parents' best efforts had accomplished little to help this child, so what could they possibly do? Still, they responded every time Fancy Free called for help.

Lindsay came home from college both the weekend we left and the weekend that we were to return. During the week in between, Nikki and Julia stayed with friends so they would not be home alone. The girls documented as well as they could the events that took place while we were out of town. Lindsay arrived home on Saturday afternoon. We had left that morning. Fancy Free's first call came at 10:30 on Sunday morning.

She wanted to know if the girls would come over to Endora's apartment and play with her, because she had no friends to play with. Lindsay asked to speak with Endora. She told Endora that she and her sisters would love to pick up Fancy Free and spend the day with her, but that she would have to bring her home by 4:00 so she could head back to school. We had left strict instructions with the girls not to let Endora know that no one would be at our home. We didn't expect them to lie, but if Endora believed an adult was staying with them during the week that would be better than her knowing that our house was empty. Joel staying with someone other than Maria and Neal could serve as ammunition in court and we feared Endora would come to the house when no one was there, or when one of the girls was there alone. Luckily, she asked no questions and agreed to the arrangement. She had errands to run, but promised to be home for Fancy Free's return at 4:00.

When Lindsay returned to our house with Fancy Free, Nikki and her friend Nita wanted to take her out to play in the snow. Endora had sent Fancy Free over in a pair of jeans and a sweatshirt, with only a windbreaker for a coat.

Six inches of snow had fallen, and it was about twenty degrees outside. So the girls found some clothes that Julia had grown out of and began to dress Fancy Free for the weather. They noticed paint all over her, the same paint Endora had used on her walls more than a week earlier. This oil-based paint would not wash off with soap and water.

At 4:00, Endora was not at her apartment. An hour later she still hadn't returned, so Lindsay took her back to our house to feed her dinner. While she was eating, Endora called to apologize. Her car had broken down. When Lindsay loaded her back into the car, Fancy Free burst into tears.

A couple of days later, Nikki came home to get the mail and check for messages. Fancy Free had left three, the third time crying and begging for Lindsay to come get her. Nikki was upset, she could hear a man in the background, and Fancy Free was not happy about his presence. So Nikki called Lindsay at school, and Lindsay called Endora to ask after Fancy Free. Endora made light of the tears on the answering machine, but Lindsay decided to come home earlier in the week than she had planned. She told Endora that she would be home the following evening and asked if she could come get Fancy Free. Endora told Lindsay that she could pick her up the next morning at 10:00 a.m.

We had called home in the meantime to get updates, and when the girls told us about the man in the background we became concerned. We knew that a woman in Endora's condition was unlikely to attract a man without issues of his own. We told Lindsay to take a male friend along to pick up Fancy Free. The next morning at 10:00, Lindsay and her friend Blaine showed up, but no one answered the door or the telephone. After half an hour had passed, they went to Blaine's apartment to see if Endora would call Lindsay's cell phone. At 11:00, she did, her excuse this time? She didn't hear them banging on the door for half an hour or the phone ringing, because her pilot light had gone out and she was messing with it. She went on to say that Fancy Free was not feeling well and was still sleeping. "Why don't you just wait until twelve to pick her up?"

Despite her worry, Lindsay waited until noon before returning to the apartment with Blaine. Fancy Free was ready to go and showed no signs of illness. Endora suggested that she spend the night with the girls, but they agreed to talk by phone later to confirm that plan. Endora babbled about off-the-wall stuff with Lindsay as if they were girlfriends. She advised Lindsay to break up with her boyfriend, Blaine's best friend, because if she didn't she would regret it by the time she was thirty and start making big mistakes. Endora claimed to be a "born-again child," eager to try all kinds of new stuff. Lindsay smiled, said "Alrighty," and thought to herself, *get me out of here.*

The weather can transform in a couple of days in this part of Missouri, so Fancy Free and Lindsay headed to the park. The melting snow had made the ground moist, so Lindsay took Fancy Free home to clean her up before dinner. When Lindsay picked her up, she saw god-knows-what encrusted in her hair, and paint on her hands, arms, and face again. Now, after playing outside, she had mud to add. While they cleaned up, Lindsay asked Fancy Free if she wanted to spend the night. For the first time, she said, "no". She had been acting strangely all day, and Lindsay was not quite sure what was going on.

Lindsay called Endora to let her know that Fancy Free wanted to come home for the night, but she wanted Lindsay to take her out for dinner and ice cream first. Endora agreed, saying she had some shopping to do. Endora was to call Lindsay at 7:00. At 7:30 she called from a Shell station. She would be home in less than half an hour. Lindsay next heard from her at 10:00 that night. After leaving the gas station, she had stopped off at a bookstore for coffee and was now "ready for Fancy Free to come home." Thirty minutes later, Lindsay arrived at the apartment with Endora's daughter, and guess what? No Endora. She showed up about twenty minutes later, at 11:00 p.m., to greet her five-year old daughter who had been "not feeling well" that morning.

Endora acted like Lindsay's girlfriend again, telling her about a guy that she met at the gas station. Actually, he owned the gas station, but that was not how he made most of his money, he also ran a porn Web site. After listening to this conversation, Fancy Free decided she would rather go home with Lindsay, and cried to hear she could not.

The next day, Saturday, Fancy Free called several times to see if we had arrived home yet. On Sunday she started again, and at least the girls could tell her that we would be home later that day. As soon as Lucas and I got into the car to drive home from the airport, around 8:00pm, we called Fancy Free. She wanted us to come get her right then. I told her I wasn't sure her mom would like that, and we were pretty worn out from traveling. By the time we got home she was on the phone again, pleading with us to come. This time I spent several minutes trying to determine whether there was something wrong, or she just missed us. Once I determined that things were all right, I promised to pick her up first thing in the morning, right after I dropped off Julia at school. She said, "You know I won't be awake." I told her to go to bed.

That evening, after twelve-year old Julia had gone to bed, Lindsay and Nikki told us all that had happened, including Endora's weird conversations with Lindsay. Up to that point, we had known the children were neglected and sometimes abused. Now we began to suspect sexual misconduct as well. Other things we noticed when Fancy Free stayed with us heightened these suspicions: She wanted to keep her panties on at bath time. She would become very angry if Lucas and I closed our bedroom door, as if she knew what we were doing and was disappointed in me. Neal and Maria noticed similar things about Joel. He was not quite three when they took him home with them, and not yet potty-trained. Every time they would change his diapers he would scream at them not to touch his penis. They never did, but it seemed someone had.

The next day, I dropped Julia at school and ran a few errands, but still called Endora by 9:30. No one answered so I left a message. No call by 2:00, so I left another message. At 3:15, after picking Julia up from school, I got a call from Fancy Free. She wanted me there now. I told her it would take about forty-five minutes for me to get there. She was very disappointed, but I told her I called twice earlier and left messages, and that she could have called me sooner. She replied, "I got up and called you first thing." A few minutes later, Endora called me back, happy and wanting to know what Fancy Free and I had planned. I let her know that I had left two messages, and she let me know that it would take her an hour to an hour and a half to get Fancy Free ready to come over. What could possibly take that long?

"Endora, if you want me to come and get her, I'm coming now. I'm not waiting and getting caught in rush-hour traffic." Endora liked to control everything, so I could feel her hair rising through the phone, but I also sensed that she was starting to have some pretty wild nights, and bet on her playing the game my way this time. The sooner I took Fancy Free off her hands, the sooner she'd be free to party.

At her apartment, I found her still angry. She informed me that in the future I should make all arrangements through her. I gave her a sarcastic grin and said, "I'm sorry, I just assumed that if a five-year old was using the phone, she was being supervised by a parent." In the car, Fancy Free revealed that her mom told her this was the last time she was going to let her come over to my house.

I suggested to Fancy Free that we go shopping and buy some clothes to keep at our house for her. That way, when she wanted to come over, she wouldn't have to pack. The voice in my head continued, *That way, your sick mom who does not work, clean, cook, read to you, or play with you won't have to inconvenience herself to pack an overnight bag for you.*

I took her to Old Navy, where she picked out a few outfits, pajamas, socks, shoes, and a sweatshirt. We went into the dressing room, I wasn't sure what size to buy. As soon as we stepped inside, she started tearing the tags off the clothes.

"Fancy Free, what are you doing?"

She looked at me kind of funny. "You know."

"No, I don't."

"I'm going to put everything on."

"Then what do you do if something doesn't fit?"

Again, she looked at me funny. I knew what was going on, but I wanted to see if she would admit it before I attempted to teach her the right way to behave. I also knew that as outspoken as Fancy Free was, the next time she shopped with her mom she was likely to pass this lesson on to her. It would send the message to Endora that we knew what she was teaching her children to do, but would also put Fancy Free in a position to be punished for doing the right thing. But I went ahead and explained to her that first we needed to try things on to make sure that they fit. If they didn't, then we had to return them to the shelves, and if there were no tags left, how would the next person know what they cost? If the clothes did fit, then we took them off and went to the front of the store to pay for them before we removed the tags. The look I get from her said, "Why would anyone do that?"

That evening when it was time for bed, Fancy Free

pulled out a diaper her mom had sent for her to wear. She already had it on when Nikki came to tell me. Way too small for her body, the diaper was cutting off her circulation. Fancy Free was a big girl for her age. I sat her down and told her that I thought it would be better if we put a trash bag between the sheet and the mattress then put a towel above the sheet. She could lie on the towel. If she had an accident, she'd come and get me, we'd put down a clean towel for her to sleep on, and I would change the linens in the morning. She expressed surprise that it would be okay to wake me up during the night. She even double-checked with my daughters. Nikki reassured her that it was okay to wake Mom up in the middle of the night if she had a problem.

The next day she and I got to spend a lot of time alone. She asked a lot of questions, and we spent quite a bit of time reading. I would read a book to her once and she could read it back to me almost verbatim. These books had moms and dads in them, so they got Fancy Free thinking. Her loyalty to her mom tugged at her, but she would occasionally stop reading and want to know if she could call Lucas "Dad." Then she would stop again and want to know if someday I would be her mom.

Endora had agreed to call me on Tuesday evening to discuss getting Fancy Free back. When I got home from picking the kids up from school, she had left two messages, one at 3:00 and one at 3:30. She was in a panic, as if we had run off with her daughter. I called her right away, and she demanded Fancy Free back "now."

"Endora, I have a life too. I have to run Julia's softball practice. When I'm through with that I will feed the kids and bring Fancy Free home. That should be around 8:00."

"No. I need her home right now, she has a dentist's appointment." I refrained from calling her a liar.

Lucas had been listening to the conversation. "Rene, I'll just take her home now."

Before she left, I told Fancy Free to tell her mom that we would take her to see her brother on the weekend, and would spend the night so they could have two days together. Endora never called, so that never happened.

Chapter Twenty-one

In mid-March, Richie returned to our house between runs. All of his work-related correspondence was being sent to our home, as he had listed it as his address. Since he still owed us a ton of money, we opened that mail, wanting to be aware of his income. The company he worked for, Reloh, kept a record of all of his phone calls, whether he was placing or receiving them. They also recorded the call's length and the other phone number. Since these records were sent to our home, we knew how often Endora called him and at what times of day. We could tell she still wasn't working she was calling Richie at all hours of the night, which meant she was sleeping all day. We also knew that her calls had to go through his company's phone system, so they were aware of the constant interruptions. He had to stop the truck when he called Endora back because of the noise. We had concerns about how long the company would put up with this and keep Richie on the payroll. When Richie returned, he expressed the same concerns, even if he tried to avoid Endora's calls, their frequency might raise flags at Reloh. But who knew what he did to egg Endora on? We never told him about the phone records his employer was sending to our home.

Richie contacted Ms. Shoffler to let her know that he

had received a letter from DFS stating that there was "probable cause on both of the children." DFS failed to explain what he was supposed to do with that information. He hoped that Ms. Shoffler would present it to the judge so that action could be taken on Fancy Free.

Once again we were disappointed. Ms. Shoffler had apparently had several meetings and conversations with Endora during Richie's time out of town. Endora could be very convincing, and had evidently succeeded in changing Ms. Shoffler's mind regarding Joel's situation. Endora's argument, "I'm the mother and I want my son. You have given my son to his father, but all he did was give Joel to someone else to take care of. If Richie is not the one taking care of him then I should have him." On the surface this is a logical argument. But Ms. Shoffler somehow forgot that Endora wouldn't take care of her son even if she got him back.

Ms. Shoffler informed Richie that she would be dropping by to visit Endora on Tuesday and would assess the living conditions in her apartment. If they satisfied her, she intended to return custody of Joel to his mother. She had told Endora the time of this visit, so it seemed an easy test, but Endora still didn't pass. What Ms. Shoffler saw appalled her. Still, she told Endora that she would return on Saturday to check again. Of course, when she did, Endora had cleaned the place.

I can't describe the fury this aroused in us. Richie's real motives were always a mystery, but he acted angry, too. Ms. Shoffler had given this very educated woman the answers to the test by telling her when she would visit, and

Endora had still failed. Now she was being given a second chance even though Ms. Shoffler's job was to protect Joel, not his mother. Later we would find out that DFS worked exactly the same way: they always called the parents to let them know when they were coming. They didn't have the time or enough caseworkers to show up for a surprise check only to find that no one was home. Never mind that a caseworker could call the home from a cell phone when they happened to be in the neighborhood, then drive up the street and drop in. Salespeople and real-estate agents do it all the time.

Richie decided to visit Endora. We never really trusted Richie, partly because he often told us he was going to check on Fancy Free but nothing ever resulted from those visits. He and Endora ended up fighting every time. Why did he put himself through that? We wondered if Endora was using sex to try to lure Richie back in, he wouldn't turn the offer down, but when Endora realized he was still not giving in on Joel she would go crazy. Then the fighting ensued and Fancy Free would witness everything. When they were moving from hotel to hotel she probably witnessed more than fighting.

On March 18, DFS appeared at Endora's apartment. At some point when Richie had been on the road, Endora had, in a fit of rage, hot lined a sexual abuse charge against him. Fancy Free vehemently denied it, so DFS never investigated further, as far as I know. Fancy Free called our house three times during DFS's visit, wanting to know if we sent them. Richie had just informed us the night before about the charges, so perhaps he called and asked them to go check on Fancy Free. Each time she called, I tried to reassure her that DFS had come to look in on her and try to protect her, just as I had told her before about the police. Endora couldn't stand bowing to authority figures, and had taught the kids to see them as enemies.

The next hearing took place two days later. Richie's attorney warned us that Ms. Shoffler planned to recommend to the judge that Joel go back to Endora, and that the judge almost always ruled according to the guardian's recommendation. The court was too backed up to listen to any other testimony. We all showed up anyway, praying that some miracle would inspire this judge to at least listen to what we had to present. Once again only Richie and his attorney, Endora and her attorney, and Ms. Shoffler were allowed in the judge's chambers. When they came out we were informed that we had to turn Joel over to Endora by 5:00 that evening.

One of two things had just happened in that judge's chambers which one, we will never know for sure. Either Richie and his attorney, whose bills we were paying, just rolled over or the system failed horribly. Here's what we know for sure: Endora gave Ms. Shoffler a note on letterhead from a cab company stating that she had been working full-time for them for ten days. No one from the court ever called to verify this or ask who would be taking care of Fancy Free if Endora were working full-time. We had brought a folder full of bad checks Endora had written all over town, as well as the letter from DFS stating that there was "probable cause for concern." Before the hearing, Richie acted as though he was going to make an argument on those issues. Since he had practiced as a criminal trial attorney, one would think he could convince a judge. Also, nothing had been done about the car that had not been inspected that Endora continued to drive the kids around in. Finally, before they went into chambers we had told Ms. Shoffler that we had a tape of all of Fancy Free's answering-machine messages in which she cried for us to please come and get her.

Ms. Shoffler informed us before going into the judge's chambers that she did not have time to listen to the tape. She apparently did not have time to check out Endora's job with the cab company either. We verified later that day that they had never even heard of her, but Ms. Shoffler would not take our calls, so we were forced to return Joel that evening. We took him to dinner, and then drove to Endora's. When she hugged him, he just hung limply. I told Endora that she had better take care of him; she responded with a smart-mouthed remark. I said that she had won the game but not the match, and that we would never stop fighting for the kids as long as she chose not to take care of them.

We spent the better part of the following week trying to get in touch with Ms. Shoffler. Suddenly she was always out of her office or in a meeting. We were not even transferred to her voicemail.

Within a week, however, Ms. Shoffler realized that she had made a big mistake. On Friday, she called to informed Lucas that if he could get Richie back in town before the court closed for the weekend she would turn custody of Joel back over to him. We didn't know what Endora had pulled to make Ms. Shoffler reverse her conclusion, she had refused to listen to us before, but the final blow came when Endora told her that she was leaving the state. Even though Ms. Shoffler had turned Joel back over to Endora, she was still his legal guardian and could not allow Endora to take him out of Missouri. The only helpful information Ms. Shoffler would give us was that Endora was in a hotel somewhere in another part of town. God was with us as, this just happened to be the area where I grew up.

Endora had been evicted from the apartment soon after she took Joel home. Not surprisingly, Ms. Shoffler or DFS had not talked with the building manager or any of her neighbors. Endora mentioned to Richie that she had left the apartment for good, and when he told us we got on the phone with the manager and the neighbors.

The manager was concerned for his job, as he had indeed been conned by Endora. It seems the landlord lived out of town and the manager had been under pressure to get the place leased. Endora came along and spun a story convincing him that he would get all the money he needed by April. By the middle of March he had not seen a cent, and began to worry. When he checked in on the place he knew he was in trouble, it was trashed and the wood floors ruined. He would have to spend hundreds if not thousands of dollars just to make the place rent able again.

Endora's neighbors told us they suspected problems but were afraid to get involved. They often saw the kids playing on the city streets with no supervision. When the furniture company showed up to repossess the items that

Endora had paid for with a bad check, their truck almost hit Joel when he ran out from between two parked cars. They went to the door and pounded, through the window, they could see Endora sleeping even as her three-and five-year olds played in the city street. The neighbors had witnessed other similar scenes, but Endora's instability scared them away from coming forward.

When the manager told Endora to get out, she threatened to have her lawyer put pressure on him for trying to evict a woman with children. Lucas got him to admit that, fearing what the apartment would look like if he allowed her to stay another month, he had actually paid her to move out. Once again, Endora left everything behind, in the dumpster out back. She must not have gotten her payoff right away, as the neighbors could see her and the kids sleeping in the car under the carport for a couple of nights.

As soon as Lucas got off the phone with Ms. Shoffler, he called Richie, who happened to be heading toward Missouri. I drove up to the area of town where Ms. Shoffler had told us Endora was staying and located Endora's motel in no time. She must have been worried that people were looking for her, she had just checked out of one location and moved across the street to another. Either that or she got kicked out. Lucas picked up Richie and headed to the courthouse while I staked out the motel. Maria and Neal headed for town. When they arrived, Neal joined the other men and Maria came to sit with me. Later that evening the guys headed to the local police station with a court order. Maria and I took our eyes off the hotel door and Endora's car only long enough to get something to eat. Even then, we sat in a booth in a Denny's from which we could see Endora's car. She almost caught us: we were so intent on watching the car that we didn't notice Endora and the kids walking right in front of the window, on their way to eat at Denny's.

While Endora was distracted chasing the kids, Maria and I slid off our seats and onto the floor. With our backs to the window, we made our way to the ladies' room. The waitress saw us, and we motioned her inside and explained the situation. She left to get our bill, promising to keep Endora away from the restroom. We slipped outside and moved the van to a spot from which we could watch them inside Denny's, which the kids proceeded to almost destroy.

Later the local police, along with Richie, showed up at the hotel to take Joel. To avoid a domestic dispute, one officer went inside, picked up Joel, and brought him out to Richie, leaving Endora crying and Fancy Free on the sidewalk, left behind again, begging the police to take her too. They never attempted to find out why.

Chapter Twenty-two

Neal and Maria took Joel on vacation with them, traveling for a week and a half by RV to Destin, Florida, and camping on the beach. They experienced the joy of seeing Joel's first reaction to the beach and the ocean. They tried to get the most out of the trip, knowing that when they returned, the chances were good that they would have to say good-bye to Joel again. Lucas had gotten the impression from Richie that Endora was wearing him down and that he might drop the divorce suit and return to her.

Meanwhile, Endora had fled to Illinois with Fancy Free. She knew that she had made the wrong move with Ms. Shoffler, and feared that DFS would not be far behind to take Fancy Free. For the next couple of months she would jump from one hotel to the next, across the state of Illinois.

She may have been avoiding DFS, but she was constantly on the phone to Richie. We could hear the exasperation in his voice when he told us that Endora called him at all hours of the day and night, crying, then screaming in anger, then crying again. He feared he would lose his job. We feared he would give up the fight and let her have Joel back. We convinced him that taking the car from Endora the next time he came home would help

at his next court appearance. The car was Richie's, actually, Lucas paid for it, but it was titled in Richie's name.
He had left the car with Endora to improve her chances
of getting a job and getting her life together, neither of
which had happened after five months. In addition, the
car's condition had worsened during those five months,
putting Fancy Free in even more danger. Our mechanic
could inspect it and prepare a written report to show the
court just how bad off the car was.

When Richie got back into town, he and I staked out
Endora's hotel in Illinois. We saw her return, and then
waited until we thought she was in for the night. Then
Richie went over and drove away in the car. The next day,
Endora called Richie, ready to explode. Meanwhile, we
took the car to our mechanic, explained the situation and
told them we wanted a detailed report for the judge and
GAL. We still held out hope that they might listen.

Later in the day, the mechanic gave us a call, asking if
he could put a "bug bomb" inside before he performed his
inspection. It was that filthy.

Endora had been pestering not only Richie, but also
her probation officer. Her five-year probation was scheduled to end the last day of May. After that, Endora would
be free to leave the state. Her probation officer already
didn't seem to know or care that she was in Illinois. We
knew that she would head back to Alabama, so we contacted the probation officer to see if the probation period
could be extended due to Endora's arrests for shoplifting
and the outstanding warrants for all the bad checks she
had written. We explained that the children would be bet-

ter protected in the Missouri, and it would give DFS more time to build a case for the children. The probation officer told us that as soon as Endora's probation period ended, she was free to go, as the officer was tired of her.

"She is just nuts, and I don't want to deal with her anymore."

Richie soon stunned us with the news that Endora had been offered a job at a clinic in Birmingham. Working as a physician. We contacted Ms. Shoffler, who took the time to call the clinic administrator to verify that they had actually hired her. She was unable to tell these people that they were making a big mistake without opening herself up to a lawsuit. The clinic was aware that Endora's license had been suspended due to her fraud conviction, but they were likely unaware of her other pending legal problems. Until they helped her get her license back, another physician would remain in the room with her at all times.

The next stunner from Richie: he intended to give Joel back to Endora now that she had a great job. Her salary of $75,000 a year would enable her to afford a place to live and good childcare. Richie would be able to visit them in between his runs instead of coming to our house. They were all going to live happily ever after. Right. Lucas tried to talk some sense into Richie, but the old arrogant know-it-all had returned, and had convinced himself that money was the answer to all of their problems. Richie was going to drop the divorce action against Endora, and we would have to return Joel.

Neal and Maria brought Joel to us on the way back from Florida. They said a tearful good-bye, with Joel unaware that his life was about to turn upside down again. We felt like we were pulling a fast one on him.

With Richie still on the road, Joel stayed with us for almost a week, and Lucas and I really got to know the little guy for the first time, he was no longer just a reminder of Richie. Lucas continued to try to get through to Richie, but Richie just got irritated that Lucas would try to tell him what to do with his son.

In the meantime, we uncovered some evidence that sickened us all.

Lucas had a chance to search the car when Richie wasn't around, a grotesque experience due to its condition. We hoped to find proof of the illegal activities we were sure Endora was involved in. Lucas found three journals that Endora had kept. Her writings would have been enough to convince anyone that she was unstable, but that soon became unimportant.

Endora had allowed Fancy Free to draw in these journals wherever she wanted. That in and of itself was strange, but it was the pictures Fancy Free drew that prompted us to call the police.

On several pages in each journal, Fancy Free had drawn men with large, erect penises. One picture, between two that Fancy Free had drawn, was obviously created by Endora. In that image, the man had an exposed erect penis, but was wearing a suit, tie, and glasses. The suit included a lapel and pockets, the kind of details a five-year old would never include. It was as if a mother and daughter had sat and drawn the pictures together. And Richie was a suit-and-tie man who wore glasses. The worst part:

on the inside of one back cover we found the address of a porn website, in Endora's handwriting. It read "*lickalicka. com* . . . Username: "fancyfree." After the unusual behavior Maria and I had witnessed during the children's bath times, this was the final straw. We prayed now that we could get the police to listen to us before Endora left the state with both children.

The police came to our house within the hour. We explained the whole story to the officer and gave him the journals. He was very concerned and took all of them with him to give to a detective, who he said would contact with us soon. The detective called within a couple of days. She asked us if the little girl would tell the judge what was happening to her. We told her we were doubtful, and she said that we would never be able to get a judge to do anything without the child describing the perpetrator's actions. What five-year-old could stand before a judge and talk about those things? Once again the authorities had let us down.

The police officer that had come to our house did have a suggestion. He said that Endora had been calling the station, asking them to make us return Joel to her. With Richie back on her side, she felt entitled. The officer said that he would try to convince her to come to the station to discuss it. If she actually crossed back into Missouri and walked in, he could arrest her for the outstanding warrants. Then he could call DFS in to take custody of Fancy Free. Finally, someone was willing to manipulate the system to actually make it work for the kids. Endora was too smart, though, she never showed up at the station.

In addition to contacting the police I wrote a letter to Ms. Stoffler, and enclosed photocopies of several pages from the journals. I knew she could do little to help Joel or Fancy Free now, with Endora living in Illinois and planning to leave for Alabama. But I hoped that she and DFS could put together a file and forward it to the Birmingham authorities. If the Division of Human Services in Birmingham had this information in hand, perhaps they would open a case file on Endora as soon as she arrived. That turned out to be wishful thinking, since no laws exist in the United States to insure that one state shares information with another state in order to protect innocent children. I am not sure if Ms. Shoffler ever did anything with this letter:

5/21/02

Dear Ms. Shoffler,

This letter is an attempt to get information to you that we have recently discovered. When we found this material Endora was living in Illinois. So we knew that Missouri's county or city DFS would not be interested in this information. We have no idea where Endora is currently, so we thought you might be able to use or forward this to anyone who may be able to assist in the safety of Fancy Free.

As you know Endora had been driving around in Richie's car, which is uninsured and unlicensed. Since it is a late model (1989) we felt that this should be viewed as possibly child endangerment as the car hadn't been inspected for over a year. Richie was aware of this but felt that if Endora was to have any chance of getting a job and getting back on her feet she would need this vehicle. Even though he chose to overlook this we still reported this to DFS, the police, her federal probation officer, and you. No one seemed to care very much and so nothing was ever done about this. After the last court appearance Richie decided that Endora had had five months to use the car to get a job, proper housing, and childcare. She had chosen to do none of the above, so he took the car back.

Lucas and I took the car to our local mechanic to have it inspected. Prior to doing this, though, we went through the car. This was no easy task because the condition of the interior was at best appalling. The filth and stench was so bad that the mechanic called to ask permission to put a bug bomb in the car before getting into it and inspecting it. The fact that these children have had to live out of this car for at least one night is reprehensible.

Lucas and I found three of Endora's notebooks in the car. I have enclosed copies of some of the information that was found in these. The pictures that Fancy Free has drawn were mixed right in the notebooks with Endora's notations. I know that Endora has made accusations to DFS regarding sexual molestation by Richie on these children. Maria and I have suspected for a while that something was not right in regards to this area. Our suspicions were based strictly on the behavior of both Joel and Fancy Free during their bath times, not anything that they had ever said. Therefore, we kept our thoughts to ourselves rather than accuse anyone of something this serious. We still do not know who is responsible for their behavior, as Endora has accused Richie. However, when we found the notation in Endora's notebooks in her handwriting regarding a web site called licklicka.com we became very concerned that maybe the accuser is not so innocent. In addition, the pictures drawn by Fancy Free of stick figures with a penis I think would be of concern to any child psychologist. The fact that the username, as noted, is fancyfree caused us even greater concern. There was one other time in March when Lucas and I were out of town that Endora called and asked our daughter, Lindsay, to come over to get Fancy Free for a while. When Lindsay took Fancy Free back that evening Endora started talking to Lindsay about child pornography web sites and what a lucrative business this was.

Please understand that we are not trying to accuse Endora of anything specifically. We are just saying that based on this information and our observation something sexually is not right with these children. If this gives you cause for concern, please do not hesitate to call us. Taking children away from their parents is obviously a very serious decision. However, the alternative, to ignore this, could be devastating for these children. Ms. Shoffler, if there is some reason that you, or the court, are not comfortable with Lucas and I or Neal and Maria that is okay. We still don't understand why the children cannot be placed in foster care until it can be determined whether or not their current environment is safe.

If you would like any information regarding the observations that Maria and I have made or have any suggestions about what we should do with this information please don't hesitate to call any of us. I would like to thank you in advance for your time.

Sincerely,
Rene Howitt

We never did tell Richie what we found. I have never ruled him out as a suspect in the abuse of Fancy Free. I never witnessed any behavior that would indicate that he was capable of this, but as time passed I trusted him less and less. After all, he gave up the fight only because "Endora was just wearing me out with all her phone calls. I'm going to lose my job," and "Everything will be all right now that Endora has this great job." Of course, he knew that money and a job were not going to cure Endora's mental illness. What was he hiding?

Later in the week, Richie pulled up to our house in a cab. He got out and had the cab driver stay, then walked in without even knocking. He took Joel right out of my arms.

"Richie, do you actually believe that any amount of money that Endora makes will be the answer to her problems?"

"Yes."

"Richie," I said, "when you came to Missouri you had a salary of ninety thousand dollars a year. Your brother has given you more than fifty thousand in the past two years. Has that made any difference for these children?"

He just stared at me. Then he said in his most pompous voice, "Endora will have her career back and I will be able to supervise the children."

"How are you possibly going to be able to supervise the care of the children when you are working as an over the road truck driver?"

He stared again. "The children will be fine." Then he turned, walked out the door without as much as a good-bye got in the cab, and left.

Lucas got in his car and followed Richie up to Wal-Mart, where Richie met Endora. He got out of the cab and handed Joel to her. She put him in her newly rented car and immediately headed for Illinois. The following day she left for Alabama to start a new life, getting away from the Howitt family and their schemes to take her children away. She loved her children and wanted them and we should have just left her alone. If Endora had been right and we had been wrong, the story would end here. But it doesn't.

PART TWO

Chapter Twenty-three

Endora's departure from Missouri with the children devastated us. We knew that things would be all right for a time, while Endora remained on a high. She had gotten a job at a clinic working as a physician and she had gotten her son back. She should have seen this as the chance to get away and start over, to escape the evils that had plagued her in Missouri. My feeling was God had just given Endora the second chance gift. Had she learnt anything? Was she capable of using these past bad life choices, penalties, and nearly loosing her children indefinitely as lessons for better decision making in the future? Was she emotionally healthy enough to even recognize this gift from God?

As for Richie, we had made it clear that if he returned Joel to his mother, we would no longer help him in any way. He planned to visit Endora in Alabama between runs instead of us, but the trucking company didn't look kindly on him changing his home base, they needed him for runs that originated in Missouri. He took as many runs as he could to avoid the problem, but at some point he either quit or was fired. After the day he took Joel from my arms, we didn't speak to him again for more than six months.

Since we had not trusted Richie for a while, the thought

actually occurred to all of us that if we had treated Endora unfairly, if she was really just a victim of circumstance, this was her chance to prove it. Her new job in her home state paid $75,000 a year, a salary that should be enough to support her and the children. She had not regained her license to practice medicine, but if she did good work and stayed out of trouble the administrators at the clinic would help her get it back permanently.

After much thought, we decided to find out where she would be living and working, then contact Birmingham's Division of Human Services to inform them of what had gone on in Missouri. We would provide Gale Shoffler's name and phone number and ask them to check on the children at least once after Endora had settled in to her new home. If they felt that she was on the right track, we would back off.

Gale Shoffler told us the name and phone number of the clinic, though it was information she was not supposed to divulge. I believe that she knew the system had failed the children terribly, and so had she. Since Richie's phone records continued to come to our home, we were able to obtain a phone number for Endora. Calling it told us that her new residence was another long-term hotel, sort of a small suite for people in transition or away from home for a long period. In late July 2002 we contacted DHR in Birmingham, Alabama. I talked with a Jaylene Golden, who worked as an intake worker. When someone called with information regarding suspected abuse, she would record that information, then relay it to someone higher up the chain of command, at which point it became a case with a caseworker assigned.

Jaylene explained all of this to me on the phone that day. I told her that I would not be following up, as our family really did want to give Endora a chance at a new start. However, we were not confident enough in her ability to do that to just let the matter drop completely. So this was our "for your information" call. If the state of Alabama cared more about Fancy Free and Joel than Missouri did, then someone would at least contact Gale Shoffler to verify the information. And perhaps that someone might feel compelled to check in on the children once or twice.

It took until September for them to assign the facts to a caseworker. DHR first had to verify that Endora was living and working at the places we had told them about. This would have needed to be handled delicately due to privacy laws. The delay was longer than we expected, but if it had enabled them to keep things under wraps, we figured it was worth the wait. Jaylene informed me that the caseworker's name was Toni Murray. They contacted me, as we were determined to remain uninvolved after the initial phone call unless we received evidence of further neglect. Ms. Murray then contacted me to let me know that she would take the time to visit Joel and Fancy Free. I cautioned her to be wary, because Endora was intelligent and educated and seemed to know just how far she could push the system. If she reached the breaking point, she would just bolt in the middle of the night with the kids. Ms. Murray felt that Endora's new job made this less likely to happen, she wouldn't want to lose it. I had to agree, but still stressed the need for the visit to be unannounced so she could get an accurate view of the situation. She assured me, in no uncertain terms, that her visit would be a surprise. "We will handle this better than Missouri did."

A couple of weeks passed, and I decided I should at least follow up this far. So I called her. She had been to visit the kids and found them to be doing just fine. But something in her voice didn't ring true.

"Was this a surprise visit?"

"Well, I tried that, and the front desk had orders from Endora not to let anyone come to her room." Instead of contacting the police, despite everything she'd been told, she went back to her office and set up an appointment with Endora. Naturally Endora passed the inspection.

At that point I realized that we had done all that we could do, Alabama was handling the situation just as Missouri had. Disappointed but resigned, we knew that the only way to help the children now was through an act of God.

Chapter Twenty-four

As October approached, Maria and I talked often about our conflicting feelings. In our hearts we knew that the kids were suffering, but we simply didn't know what more to do. Doing nothing took more discipline than either of us knew we had. At times, the four of us talked about getting into the car and taking off for Alabama.

We could tell by Richie's phone records that Endora's constant calls had resumed. They were being made during the afternoon and into the early morning hours, from her home number, so we knew that things at work were not going well. If they were, she would be at the clinic in the afternoons and she certainly wouldn't be staying up until 3:00 a.m. Stewart's words kept coming back to us: "She will never be able to keep a job longer than three months." Since she had started this job in the beginning of June, if Stewart was right, by September she would be struggling. It was now October.

One Friday afternoon that month, I came home from a tennis match to find a strange message on my answering machine. A lawyer in Arkansas urgently wanted to know if we were related to a Joel Howitt. What could it possibly be about? As far as I knew, Endora and the kids still lived in Alabama.

When I returned his call, the lawyer told me that a friend of his had daily contact with Fancy Free and Joel and what she had witnessed concerned her deeply. She did not know what to do or who to call so she contacted him, as he was a family friend who happened to practice family law. She wanted to remain anonymous, so he would not give me her name. He had found us through the court system in Missouri, since Joel had once had an Order of Protection assigned to him.

I explained the whole story, including the fact that Endora had fled back to Alabama as soon as legally possible. He told me that there was a person who went to Endora's home each morning, got the kids out of bed and ready, and took them to school. All while Endora slept. I suspected this person and his anonymous person were one and the same, but did not push for her name. I did ask the attorney to have his friend contact DHR and report what she had seen to Toni Murray. Before we hung up, I managed to learn the name and phone number of the kids' school.

I immediately called Maria. It was 3:00 on Friday afternoon, so we would need to move fast if we were going to find out anything before the weekend. We agreed that Maria would contact the school and I would contact DHR. Maria had much more luck than I did, by 3:00 DHR was already shutting down for the day, and without a clear emergency the intake person refused to contact Toni Murray. I needed concrete evidence of something going on that day, otherwise no one would check on the kids over the weekend.

Maria called the Sacred Mother School to find that it was both a preschool and a kindergarten. Fancy Free was at kindergarten age, and Joel still in preschool. After a long conversation with the principal, Maria learned that the school had been concerned for several months. Everything she told Maria had to be strictly off the record, as that kind of information was legally private. But the principal felt great compassion for the two children, and after Maria explained what we had been through and our futile attempts to help them, she began to tell her story.

The school had long suspected serious problems involving Endora, but Endora had always had an explanation, and since she was a doctor they gave her the benefit of the doubt. Still, the school had reported the situation to DHR. Did DHR ever do anything? The school did not know.

The state of Alabama does not require kindergarten; however, if you enroll your child in it they must follow the same attendance guidelines required by the state for all other grade levels. During the first forty-two days of the school year, Fancy Free was absent or tardy thirty times. School officials had called Endora in and talked with her about the situation several times, but she had gotten away with the excuse of being a doctor on call and a single parent. It finally reached a point where the law required the school to report the problem. In addition to the attendance issues, they had required medical records for enrollment, just as Maria had needed for Joel's daycare. Endora had told the school that she was in the process of getting copies of these records, but that she did not have them at present because everything had been lost in a house fire. As the situation declined, the school realized this was probably a lie too.

The school was separated into two parts, the elementary school and the preschool. Each had a separate principal, and the two discussed Joel and Fancy Free with each other. It became apparent that they were noticing the same things, indicating a problem in the home: both children regularly showed up at school hungry, tired, and unkempt. Joel would stuff as much food into his mouth as possible when they served lunch or snacks, as if storing up. Both the kids were very cautious about what they said, but had talked about Neal, Maria, Lucas, and Rene. Joel had gone on and on about Dan, Dave, and Dewayne, Neal and Maria's boys, who had become like brothers to him. The school thought perhaps these had been foster families from the past. Finally they told Endora that the children must come to school on time and on a regular basis, or they would have no choice but to expel them. That must have been when Endora hired a caretaker to come get the kids ready for school every morning.

Maria and I got nothing accomplished on Friday, even though one of the principals gave Maria her home number and actually went over to the DHR office and knocked on doors to try to get someone to listen. The doors were locked. The next day our family had plans to meet Neal and Maria in Columbia, Missouri, to watch the state high-school softball finals. Between games we went out to lunch. The only conversation between the four of us all day had been about the kids, so Maria called the principal at home to get an update. Apparently, Endora had been admitted to the hospital for an emergency procedure on her gall bladder. No one knew the kids whereabouts. So Maria called to see if someone from DHR would go with the police to Endora's hotel suite to see if the children were all right, and make sure they hadn't been left there alone with no food or supervision. What if there had been a fire? We knew that they had been left alone before. Maria relayed this information to the intake worker, and told her about this being an open case and that the school principal would verify her concerns.

"Ma'am, it sounds as though your biggest concern is that the children have food for the weekend, and neglect is not an emergency. So we will not be able to go and check on the children until Monday."

I flashed back to December, when I'd been told by DFS, "Ma'am, if you haven't been in the house and actually seen the condition, then we can't come out to check on them." Did they all go to the same school for idiots? If these children had been part of their families, would they have acted the same way?

On Monday I called DHR and left a message for Toni Murray. She never returned that call or any of my follow-up calls.

A couple of weeks had passed since the call from the attorney in Arkansas. Maria was keeping in contact with one of the school principals, she seemed to care about the children as much as we did, initiating several of the phone conversations. The bad news came: Endora had stopped bringing the children to school, left the hotel, and been fired from her job. And we knew that Richie had lost his income, since the phone records from the trucking company stopped arriving at our house. We now had no way to track the kids, so we just started praying.

Chapter Twenty-five

On December 24, 2002, I found myself thinking of the previous Christmas Eve and our visit to the kids. Since the end of October we had not heard a word from Richie or had any news about the kids. I consciously decided to try to avoid thinking about it, as it just brought me down. Lucas was out with every other man in the world: at the mall, doing last minute Christmas shopping. Living with four women, he was pretty used to the annual teasing he had to take for this seemingly gender-related activity. By three o'clock we were all home and ready for the evening. A snowstorm had just hit the area and we sat in the family room discussing whether to change our usual tradition of going out on Christmas Eve. Lucas got up to answer the phone, and when he walked back into the room I knew immediately that something was up.

Richie had called to say that he was headed for Missouri and was about four hours away. He had the kids with him but not Endora. We didn't know the details, but they didn't matter much. We suddenly realized that we had no Christmas gifts for the kids. Richie and Endora surely didn't buy them anything. The girls and I drove to Wal-Mart in the snowstorm, with little time before it closed at six o'clock. The four of us dashed up and down the aisles, grabbing anything the kids might enjoy out of what remained on the shelves. Then we headed for the grocery store, when Neal and Maria heard the news, they were sure to change their plans and head to our house on Christmas Day.

When we got home Lucas had talked with Maria but had no luck getting a hold of Richie for additional information. The five of us spent the next hour putting away all of the presents that had sat under the tree for weeks, wrapping the new ones, and then finding places to hide them. We didn't know what Joel and Fancy Free had been told about Santa. Since Richie's ETA was a mystery, Lucas decided to stay home to wait for them. The girls and I drove across the street to church for Christmas Eve services.

We'd been home from church for a short time when Richie pulled up with the kids at around eight o'clock. The snow had really piled up, and the kids hopped out of the car supercharged, between being here for Christmas and the snow. We could see that Richie felt like a hero for doing this for the kids. We, on the other hand, are sickened by the fact that they have had to endure another six months of turmoil and neglect. Things must have really gotten out of hand again for Richie to come running back to us after his grand departure.

Joel and Fancy Free ran off with our girls to play upstairs, giving us a chance to speak to Richie. Before he even had a chance to start explaining what led up to this, Lucas announced that Endora and the police had called several times. Endora claimed that Richie ran off with the kids while she was sleeping, an easy feat, since she slept all day. Lucas was honest with her, saying that Richie had called and might be on his way to our house. He assured her that the call had come with no warning. In fact, Lucas had not talked with his brother since he came to our home in May and took Joel. Endora, in her normal state of paranoia, refused to believe him and contacted the police, who in turn called our home. Lucas suggested to Richie that he contact the police immediately and let them know that he was at our house with the kids. Richie actually listened.

When the police arrived, they had spoken with Endora several more times. They also remembered Endora's behavior in May, and the circumstances surrounding the situation. But they needed to see the kids to know that they were all right. So our girls brought them downstairs. As soon as the police saw their excited moods, they contacted Endora to let her know that they were indeed here, happy and unharmed. Endora wanted Richie arrested for kidnapping, claiming that Richie took Fancy Free without her consent. Richie, on the other hand, said that he and Endora discussed their situation until Endora fell asleep, and they had mutually decided that the kids would be better off in Missouri with us for a while. He took the kids while Endora was sleeping because he knew how quickly Endora could change her mind and didn't want to give her the chance. They had both decided that he should bring the kids to us and then return to Alabama. Having dealt with Endora in the past and seeing that the kids were happy, the police decided not to arrest Richie and take the kids into custody on Christmas Eve. They told Endora that she knew the kids would be taken care of and could deal with all of this after Christmas.

Chapter Twenty-six

Lucas and I got up first on Christmas morning. We didn't need to worry about Joel and Fancy Free being up and wired, since neither of them had ever experienced a normal Christmas. Their minds weren't swimming with visions of stockings full of candy and beautifully wrapped presents spread out under a lit-up tree, or of soft Christmas music and the smell of home-baked cinnamon rolls. I have often wondered what children like them think when they see Christmas scenes on television and Santa at department stores, things they never see at home. Joel and Fancy Free had no knowledge of the meaning of Christmas. Maria and Lucas had exposed Joel to Sunday school while they had him, but never during Christmas. This would be our second Christmas morning with Fancy Free, but she had no memory of the first one, as she had been only two years old.

After Lucas and I set out all of the gifts, our daughters woke Joel and Fancy Free. They were confused, why would anyone get up this early? When they came downstairs Fancy Free sprang to life but Joel still didn't know what to think. It hadn't dawned on him that any of the gifts were for him. The blessing for us was that our girls couldn't have cared less about their own presents. The joy of watching Joel and Fancy Free tear into presents and then play with them was all they needed.

A couple of hours later Neal and Maria arrived with Dewayne and his girlfriend, and the festivities began again. Joel went crazy with joy at the sight of them. But even at the ages of three and six, we could see the questions in their eyes: When is this going to end? When do we go back to reality?

Later, after Maria and I got dinner started, we sat in the dining room to discuss what would happen tomorrow. Eventually our husbands joined us, and then Richie. We asked him point blank, "What happens next?" He informed us that Endora had a job prospect, at a rural hospital in Alabama that had a hard time attracting doctors. He intended to leave tomorrow without the kids, but he didn't want us to separate them. His plan was to go back to Alabama and take Endora for her final interview. After she officially had the job, he would work on getting a place to live and furnishing it. Then he would come back for the kids and take them to Alabama. He planned to be a stay-at-home parent; a stable force in their lives while Endora brought home paychecks. He promised to see that she stayed in therapy and took her medicine.

Our first question: "What if Endora doesn't get this job?" Richie's mind hadn't crossed this bridge, but he felt sure she'd be hired. We looked at each other in bewilderment. He still didn't get it. Endora had managed to get her license back with the help of her last employer, but they eventually fired her. Any new prospect would see that and have access to the fact that she had previously lost her license. None of us thought Endora would be any employer's first choice, based only on her employment record. We didn't even want to imagine how she would look in an interview.

Next question: "How long do you anticipate all of this will take?" His response? "About two weeks." He elaborated on how he would accomplish everything so quickly and we just listened. Then it was our turn to talk. We explained to Richie that none of his plans would happen as easily as he anticipated, and even if they were, he hadn't fully considered the details. For example, Fancy Free should be in school. In the state of Missouri a child her age was required to be enrolled in kindergarten. And what if they got sick or hurt? Richie could give us a letter of consent to treat Joel, but not Fancy Free. His take was that they had no insurance anyway, so why did it matter? He never did address the school issues.

We felt the need to at least introduce to Richie the potential pitfalls of staying at home with the children. Maria and I knew this man had no clue how much energy it took to stay at home all day and evening with young children. At fifty-six years old, what was Richie thinking? He had the patience of a woman in labor in rush hour traffic, and he thought he could handle staying at home with a three and a six-year old. A woman with whom he has never had a good relationship would be providing their entire income, and he thought he would control the family's finances and budget. It would have been a tough change for two normal, healthy adults, never mind these two. And it all hinged on two things Endora had been unable to accomplish so far: getting and keeping a good job, and committing to therapy and medication.

Endora called several times that day, and we knew from Richie's end of the conversation that they were discussing the arrangement. He never seemed frustrated or angry with her, so we assumed Endora had agreed to the idea of Richie leaving the children with us when he returned to her.

When we put Joel to bed that night he wanted to know if there would be presents again the next morning.

The day after Christmas, Lucas and I rose at 7:00 a.m. to find Richie gone. He left no note to us or his children, and no signature permitting Lucas and I to seek medical treatment for the kids. What would we tell Fancy Free and Joel when they awoke? We decided to wait until they asked questions. They didn't even notice his absence until dinnertime, and when we explained that he probably went back to Alabama to check on their mom, they acted like they really didn't care.

Chapter Twenty-seven

Over the next few days, the kids and I spent a lot of time together, our kids were on Christmas break, and we had no routine to follow. Still, the girls needed rides to various activities with their friends, so Joel, Fancy Free, and I were spending a lot of time in the car. For some reason, the kids began to open up to me there in the car. They had been raised to believe that questions by anyone were cause for suspicion, so we always had to wait until they choose to reveal any information. The car seemed to be the place.

The first Saturday after Christmas I took them to visit Neal and Maria. We spent the night and all went to church the next morning. Their church community was elated to see Joel again. During the two-hour drive back from Maria's, I first heard details directly from the kids about their everyday life with Endora. Maybe because the girls and Lucas were not with us, or maybe something in the music I played set them off. When they started talking to me, my heart raced and my hands gripped the steering wheel so tightly my knuckles turned white. Joel started by asking if he could call me Mommy. This didn't surprise me, as he had asked the same question of Maria when she brought him home. Immediately, Fancy Free exploded in his face. He had betrayed their mother. I could hear them whispering to each other in the backseat. That in and of itself was monumental: whispering.

One of the idiosyncrasies we always noticed about the kids was that they didn't seem to grasp the concept of volume. We assumed they spent so much time around yelling and screaming that they had to struggle to be heard by their parents or by each other. They didn't yell; they just always talked very loudly. At home, in public, at church, wherever they were, they spoke at one volume: loud.

Now suddenly I heard them whispering forcefully, obviously expressing strong opinions. After a few moments of silence, Joel spoke up.

"Rene, I said, can I call you Mom?" I peeked at Fancy Free in the rearview mirror. If looks could kill, Joel would have been bug juice on my windshield. So I told them both that they could call me whatever they felt comfortable calling me. Then I told Fancy Free not to be mad at her brother, reminding her that he was two years younger and more confused, but still knew who his real mommy was. She thought for a while, and her features softened.

Fancy Free chose that moment to tell me about the closet that she and Joel stayed locked in. Trying to avoid questions about their mom, I asked if this was some kind of game that she and Joel played.

"No, it's where we stay when Mommy is gone."

"You mean like if she has to run to the store real quick for milk?" As if this would justify it.

"No, I mean when she has to go out."

The fact that Endora left them unattended was no surprise, but the closet part made no sense to me because they had almost always lived in motel rooms whose closets don't have locks. I just said "Huh," as though thinking about it. Fancy Free seemed pensive too, until she started to tell me about getting hit. I asked where, and could see her hitting the back of her head. I knew that asking who hit them might end the conversation.

"Does it hurt badly enough to cry?"

"Yes."

Joel then spoke. "My daddy hits me."

Fancy Free didn't seem too upset by that statement, so I asked her, "Does Daddy hit you too?"

"No."

Joel says, "Mommy just hits her."

After that, Fancy Free decided to move on to another topic, but this time wanted me to guess what had been happening to her and who did it. She spoke of a voice in her head telling her to tell me "stuff," but she just couldn't do it. I believed she was referring to sexual molestation, but I couldn't be the one to refer to anything sexual first. If I did and was wrong, I could be planting a terrible idea in her head.

"Fancy Free, I can help you but you have to tell me what is happening first." In the rearview mirror I saw her shaking her head.

After a while she said, "Sometimes in my dreams. My dreams tell me to tell you."

"Honey, can you just give me a little hint of what you are talking about?"

"You know what I'm talking about." The somber look on her face said it all. "Why don't you just say it and then

I can shake my head no if you're wrong and yes if you're right."

"I can't do that, Fancy Free. It has to come from your mouth the first time." We went back and forth for at least half an hour, until we pulled into our driveway. I never did get her to be any more specific.

As soon as I had time alone I called Maria and repeated each word the kids had said. Neither of us knew what we should do with this information, but since Maria was a nurse, she decided to ask some of the doctors and nurses in the emergency room at her hospital for advice the next day. We agreed that she should tell them about Fancy Free's odd bath-time behavior too. She still hated undressing from the waist down, and wanted no part of me showering in the same room while she bathed. Joel, on the other hand, displayed no inhibitions during his bath time, and since Maria potty-trained him, the diaper was no longer an issue.

Endora called that night. I had run to the grocery store and Lucas was at home with Joel, Fancy Free, Julia and some of her friends. Endora demanded to speak to the kids. When Lucas put them on, she yelled so loudly at them through the phone that Lucas, Julia, and her friends heard every word. She commanded that they say "I love you, Mommy," but the kids didn't want to say it. Frozen, they just listened to their mother rant and rave. As Joel and Fancy Free cried, Julia and her friends and even Lucas cried. Finally he had to end the conversation.

When I walked in the door, I saw Julia's red eyes and knew something was wrong. I went upstairs to find Lucas coming out of the bedroom that was now Joel and Fancy Free's. Bedtime was a challenge, since they had stayed up for years until 3:00 or 4:00 in the morning and slept all day. During Christmas break, our girls were not going to bed early and the kids wanted to stay up with them. After being a stay-at-home mom for almost fourteen years, I knew the only way to remain sane was to set a bedtime for little ones and stick with it, no matter how long it takes or how many tears you see. So each night we started at 8:30, and by 10:00 we usually had Fancy Free sleeping. If we were lucky, Joel was out by 11:00. He took longer to get to bed, and usually slept later. We woke them at 6:30 or 7:00 in the morning in an effort to reset their internal clocks. It wasn't until two or three weeks later that we saw any positive effects.

Since Endora called after 8:30, she not only tortured them with her words but planted the experience fresh on their little minds right before bedtime. Lucas closed our bedroom doors behind him and told me what had transpired; so upset he could barely talk about it. I called Richie back. In a low and apologetic voice he said, "The police are here right now, I'll call you back as soon as they leave." I had no idea what that was about and never did ask. He called back a while later.

"Richie, neither you nor Endora will be allowed to talk with these children after 7:00 p.m. So you will just be wasting your time if you try to call. We have caller ID and we will not answer the phone."

"Understood."

"When you or Endora do call, as soon as anything

negative or upsetting is said, the conversation will be ended immediately. Is that understood?"

"Yes."

"Richie, does Endora have any idea how upsetting that whole ordeal was to everyone here? Not just her kids, but ours too, and Lucas. Does she have any concept of how a normal family functions?"

"It won't happen again."

Chapter Twenty-eight

After Christmas, the kids continued to tell me about the closet and used dolls to recreate their beatings. It became apparent that Richie was tougher on Joel and usually hit him in the rear end, but not always. Endora, on the other hand, seemed to have a shorter fuse with Fancy Free, and always hit her in the back of the head. The closet still puzzled me. Hearing that it was larger than the two walk-in closets in our bedroom made it even more confusing, as the kind of motels these kids had lived in do not generally have large closets.

Maria had consulted with the doctors and nurses in her hospital's emergency room and the general consensus was that we should take the children to the emergency room at the best children's hospital in our area. The doctors there would know what to do, and the hospital had on-staff social workers to assist them with problems such as this. Maria drove to town and we arrived at the hospital with the children at about 6:30 in the evening, having told them that we thought it would be a good idea to share some of the things they had told us with a doctor or a nurse. The flu had hit Missouri hard that year, so it was packed, and we hoped the kids didn't catch anything.

After several hours of waiting, a doctor sat down with

Maria and I to hear the whole story. He then had nurses take the children to separate rooms and asked Maria and I to wait in the hallway. He and a nurse went into each room to talk with the kids one at a time. When he returned to Maria and I, he informed us that he believed the "closet" the kids referred to was actually the motel room itself. Endora had left them all day while she worked, looked for work, or did whatever she wanted. Since her day never began until late afternoon when she had no job to go to, the kids had often been alone after dark. According to them, she left behind bread and peanut butter, with Fancy Free responsible for making the sandwiches. They got water from the sink. The doctor believed there was more going on, so he asked for permission to do physical exams. We thought that would be a good idea.

Joel couldn't have cared less. He got completely undressed and let the doctor check him from head to toe. Fancy Free undressed herself, insisting that everyone leave the room. She had draped the paper blanket over herself when the doctor and nurse came back in the room. She was all right with the exam until the doctor asked to look under her panties, which she had not removed. She went to pieces. The doctor emerged into the hall and asked me to come into the room. I tried to reassure her that everything was all right and that I would stay with her and hold her hand, but she wanted no part of it. She simply cried, with her arms crossed and her eyes throwing daggers at me.

At six years old, she should not know to be fearful of any of this. I had raised three daughters and been through countless physicals with them. I even remembered the first time that my pediatrician asked my mother if he could do a breast exam on me, at the age of thirteen. I was uncomfortable, but my mom said it was okay so I didn't question it. My daughters never responded negatively either. If I gave the doctor the okay, it was okay with them. Why would Fancy Free be hysterical at the idea?

The doctor asked me to step back into the hall with him. He told us that this was definitely a warning sign of some type of sexual abuse. Maria and I looked at each other, further support of our suspicions. The doctor didn't think we should force her to undergo the exam, but he intended to call a social worker, and they would need as much information from us as possible. The doctor, and later the social worker, talked with us about a SAMs (Sexual Abuse and Molestation) test that could tell them if she had ever been raped. He thought perhaps it should be performed later in the week, and Fancy Free should be mildly sedated to avoid further trauma. We all decided to wait until Fancy Free had settled down, and Maria and I could have a chance to think.

Maria and I went into the exam rooms and dressed the kids. We were then led to an office and introduced to a social worker. After we again related the story, she said she would talk with the doctor and contact us later that day, it was now 1:00 a.m. on December 31.

The social worker called later that morning to let me know that the doctor had hot lined the case to the county DFS, and that someone from that office would be contacting us within a couple of hours.

That call came shortly after we hung up. The caseworker and the investigator showed up at our house before noon, surprising on New Year's Eve since our previous experience with the county DFS had been less than stellar. We couldn't get them to listen or do anything on a weekday, much less a holiday, yet two women now stood in our doorway with genuine concern on their faces. They sat with us in the kitchen, and expressed a desire to meet Joel and Fancy Free and our kids, and to see the house.

Sandy Fish was the caseworker assigned to Joel and Fancy Free, and would be our contact as long as we had them in our custody. She and the investigator explained that they talked with the doctor and social worker from the hospital and pulled the file from six months earlier, when the children had previously been hot lined. They had already made the decision to take the children into protective custody and place them in foster care. If Lucas and I agreed to go to foster care classes and allow them to inspect our home, they would place the children with us, so they didn't have to take them away that day. Naturally, Lucas and I consented.

Just out of curiosity, I asked Sandy what she thought of the pictures that DFS had taken of the house Joel and Fancy Free were living in when this all started. I just had to know if she would have handled things differently had she been assigned to the case. She looked at me and said, "There were no pictures in the file."

We gave her the names of the people who had worked on the case previously. She said that she already had the names and that none of those people worked for DFS any longer. She could not tell us if they had quit or been fired. We suggested strongly that they try to find those pictures, and that Gale Shoffler might have copies. At that point those pictures and the journals were the only physical evidence we had of how extreme the situation was.

We got out the journals and showed them the pictures Fancy Free had drawn, the one Endora had drawn, and the notations about the porn website. Sandy sat for a while and read some of Endora's entries. She wanted to take all of it with her. I told her that I understood, but didn't want to let them out of my hands as it had taken Lucas and I over a month to retrieve them from the police after we lost the kids the first time. We agreed to make copies of everything in the journal for her file. Lucas and I held on to the originals.

We described to Sandy about how Neal and Maria had taken care of Joel even though Richie had custody of him. A caseworker in that area had visited Neal and Maria to investigate back in February, so there was presumably a file there too. We asked if Neal and Maria could attend the classes with us, as they wanted to help care for the kids, a tricky issue, since Neal and Maria lived outside of this jurisdiction. But we made her understand how indispensable Neal and Maria's help would be, and had been, she agreed. Sandy wanted to know up front if we would be willing to adopt Joel and Fancy Free if it came to that. So we explained the plan the four of us had come up with early on. She informed us, as Stewart had, that splitting the kids up was never the first choice. However, she understood that Joel, Neal, and Maria had already bonded, so as long as we kept the kids together and Neal and Maria took the classes, they could help us care for the kids. Moving into the adoption stage would take months, if not years, so that conversation could wait.

The home study included, Lucas and I attending a ten hour long class on a Saturday, criminal and medical background checks on every person living under our roof, and a thorough inspection of our home. All of this was required for approval as a "kinship family." The inspection started that day. Sandy told us to appear in court with the kids at 8:30 a.m. on January 2, 2003.

Chapter Twenty-nine

On January 2, our kids went back to school and we went to court, a hectic morning even if the roads weren't a mess from all the snow. We had decided not to tell Joel and Fancy Free until the last minute where we were going. After getting our daughters out the door, we sat Joel and Fancy Free down to tell them that we had to appear in court. Fancy Free felt sick to her stomach, and we knew why: each time we'd left the courthouse before, Joel had been taken away from Endora while she was left behind. Even though we assured her that wouldn't happen this time, she had no reason to believe that anything good would happen for her from getting involved with the law or the state. We tried to explain to her that if we didn't go through this process, her mother could show up at our door anytime and take her from us, even if she had no job, no place to live, no money to feed her. If she or Joel got sick, we needed permission to take them to the doctor. This helped a little, but not much. We told her that if she trusted us enough to do this, when we got home I could start working on getting her into kindergarten. That idea amazed her. Despite spending their lives locked away, both children were extremely social. And Fancy Free had a keenly intelligent mind, so the thought of actually going to school and having friends helped calm her.

The way that Richie handled the situation had made all the court proceedings exceedingly complicated. Did he kidnap the children while their mother was asleep, or had she agreed to let them go? The court had no desire to aid and abet kidnapping, so they had to remain cautious. On that day in January we never actually entered a courtroom, but statements were taken from Lucas and I, and Sandy. The report was then passed on to the judge, who did sign the necessary papers to grant custody of the kids to DFS. The agency in turn placed them with us. I believe the only thing that allowed this to happen so easily on that day was the fact that neither parent had called us since the night of the 29th, when all the shouting had taken place. It had been four full days, and we had no way to get in touch with them.

We did know that Endora didn't get the hospital job Richie was so sure about, if she had, he would have called to boast. And there was just no way any reputable place would employ her as a physician in the condition she was in. They were completely out of money and thus no longer at the hotel they last called us from. Sandy had dialed the last number they had used and verified they were no longer there. With no way of contacting the parents, the judge had no choice but to sign the papers.

Whether Richie kidnapped the kids or not was never a concern for Lucas and I, or for Neal and Maria. After losing his job, he had gone to check on the kids, maybe more to be with Endora than to be with them; it doesn't really matter. The fact is, after being back a short while, he realized things had worsened since he left the last time. We all had criticized him quite a bit then for leaving Endora to save himself but leaving the kids behind. This time we believed he thought he was doing the right thing by bringing the kids with him. He did go back to her, so we believed his story about planning to get the two of them back on their feet. But the fact that he was naive enough to believe that he could get it done in two weeks, or to ever get it done with her, was unfathomable.

We now had legal placement of the kids. I couldn't imagine what the next phone call with Endora and Richie would be like.

When we got home from court I went to work immediately on getting Fancy Free into school. She had already missed most of the first semester, and we wanted to make sure she'd be ready for the first grade by the next school year. This was no easy task, as once again we lacked her immunization records. I called the school she had attended in Alabama, but the only records they had gotten from Endora were ones that Endora herself had signed off on as the physician. Who knows if she ever actually gave any shots? The school only got those records after threatening to throw the children out of school if Endora didn't provide the necessary paperwork.

Earlier on, I had gotten the name of the pediatrician the kid's saw in Missouri through Fancy Free's preschool. I called and was told that she had passed away. Her office gave me the names of the doctors they had referred patients to, but Endora had never actually taken the kids to see the new doctor. So I was at another dead end.

I contacted our pediatrician and made an appointment

for the required physical to attend school. She could not fit Fancy Free in for several days, so I had to take her to the county clinic to start her immunizations. She was given several doses that day and it took two adults to hold her down while the doctor administered them. She was suspicious of doctors, and had overheard us discussing shots. But those shots enabled Fancy Free to start kindergarten the next day.

Chapter Thirty

Time, finally, for a normal family routine. Prior to having both Joel and Fancy Free full time, I had been able to sit at my computer at least four mornings a week, coffee in hand, opening e-mails, writing to friends and family, and documenting the events in Joel's and Fancy Free's lives. We had a high schooler, Nikki, whom I always liked to see out the door and touch base with on her schedule for the day. We had Julia, in middle school. I had always driven to school just to have extra time with her. Now I would return home from dropping her off and get Joel and Fancy Free out of bed. She always got up easily enough, but he was not a happy person in the morning, probably because he had hardly ever seen the morning. We would all head to the kitchen for breakfast and then back to the bedroom to shower and get Fancy Free ready for morning kinder- garten. I walked her up to the bus stop and sat with her until the bus pulled up. She wanted the whole nine yards: school, the bus ride, she wanted to experience it all.

My new job could have been much harder: the group of banks that Lucas had worked for had sold out to a larger group in September of 2001. Lucas hadn't planned on early retirement, but the battle for the kids had begun that December, and Richie lived with us until the following May. Lucas did not seriously consider any jobs, since he often needed to be in court or attend meetings with Richie and his attorney. In addition to that, he spent countless hours on the phone with people who called trying to track Endora. They were always recipients of her bad checks. Lucas encouraged them to file complaints with the police and on several occasions even met them at the station to help with the paperwork. After Endora fled Missouri with the children, he contacted every state agency and politician he could in an effort to understand how something like that could be allowed to happen.

When I returned home from the bus stop, Lucas would be playing with Joel or trying to get Joel interested in playing on his own so Lucas could actually get something done. My husband was living the life of a stay-at-home mom, and guess what? He was not having fun. During the previous three months, when Endora's kids were gone, Lucas and I had begun to move on with our lives. He enjoyed being at home and working on projects he had never had time for. Getting to see his kids play softball and soccer. Best of all, he and I had time together during the day to just sit and talk, something rare for married people with children. Now our lives had abruptly changed.

Endora loved to tell anyone who would listen that Lucas and I just wanted her children. Right, we just couldn't wait to give up a lifestyle that allowed me to play tennis four times a week and Lucas to golf or fish or ride his motorcycle. Sometimes we would just sit at home, I drew or painted while Lucas worked on his coin collection or played his favorite card game or dominoes on the Internet. We sometimes shared lunch, or spent the afternoon getting chores done. Of course, the chores part lasted only until it was time to run off to one of our girls' softball or soccer games. Sure, we couldn't wait to make room for Endora's four-year old and six-year old in our daily schedule.

If Lucas had still been busy with his career, I would have had to give up my entire life just because his brother decided to have one hellacious mid-life crisis. I don't honestly know if I could have taken it. As it was, we leaned on each other. Finding yourselves with two young children overnight, in your mid-forties, makes you understand why God intended us to have children while we're young. And these kids came with a lot of extra baggage. We weren't out to steal Endora's kids. But something had to be done.

Chapter Thirty-one

The week after DFS placed the kids in our home and Fancy Free started kindergarten, we finally heard from Richie, but he wasn't calling to speak to the kids. He needed us because he and Endora were broke and desperate. She hadn't gotten the job, their latest hotel had kicked them out, and something had happened that involved the police, Richie had said they were there the night of Endora's terrible phone call to the kids. They were now driving around almost aimlessly in rural indigent parts of Alabama, knowing it was the only area of the state in which Endora had any prayer of getting a job. These are areas of the state where no other doctor wanted to work or live. Having Richie along prevented Endora from engaging in any illegal activity to make money. I will say this for Richie: through all of this, as far as we could tell, he never did anything illegal to support himself or Endora. Although I do feel that in almost every other aspect of his life he has been immoral and dishonest.

So Richie called us to ask Lucas to wire him money so they could survive, putting Lucas in the worst position I have seen him in before or since. We had discussed many times with Neal and Maria the fact that our giving Richie and Endora money for so long had only enabled them to dig a deeper and deeper hole. The four of us had concluded that every time we helped Richie and Endora financially, we were hurting the kids. If we had never given Richie a dime, he would have had to make different choices from the very beginning. And different choices could have led only to better results, it was hard to imagine anything worse: a doctor and a lawyer destitute, and their children taken into custody by the county. They didn't even have the money to eat. Richie was still Lucas's brother, and we reasoned that we had the kids now, so sending something to Endora and Richie couldn't hurt them. Richie didn't ask about the kids, and we didn't tell him.

We called Maria. The conflicting emotions in Lucas and his sister were overwhelming. How could they not feed their own brother? Despite our vow, Lucas went out and wired his brother a hundred dollars. Before Lucas could even get back home, and he was only a mile away, his brother was on the phone complaining that he needed more money. They had gotten used to Lucas giving them hundreds of dollars at a time, and that's what they expected to get. We were stunned. After such a painful decision, we got a phone call to complain, not to say thank you.

Finally, the next Sunday morning, Richie called to speak to the kids. It had been about ten days since Endora's outburst of anger over the phone at them. I was the only one home; we had given the kids to Neal and Maria for the weekend. So the house was quiet.

This was the moment we had been dreading: telling Richie and Endora that DFS had taken custody of their kids and made us their foster parents. I told Richie the kids were not home.

"Richie, I have something to tell you." I said that the kids had relayed some pretty terrifying stories to us, so we had taken them to the hospital emergency room. As I told him the whole story, Richie never seemed to get upset. He just listened. I left out the details of the stories the kids had told, as this would have just given him and Endora time to come up with explanations. I gave him Sandy's name and phone number and told him to contact her, as she was trying to find them. He never did ask where the kids were, so I didn't offer to tell. Sandy had instructed us not to allow them to speak with the kids until she had spoken with each of them anyway.

Fewer than five minutes passed between this phone call and the second call, from a furious Endora. Once again, I answered the phone, with my heart was racing. I had hoped that Lucas would be the one to handle this situation. But then a calm came over me, and I just let Endora vent, as she had the day Maria and I had visited her at the hotel more than a year ago. Amazingly her first line of defense was that "I never sexually abused my children." I was thinking: *Wow, why would these be the first words out of her mouth?* When she had settled down a little, I asked her if she could, for a moment, put herself in our position. Two children had been left with us without any notice. We didn't know where their parents were, nor had they called about their children in ten days. We had no legal reason to have them. We didn't even know whether their mother approved of the situation or not.

"What were we to do if the kids got sick or hurt? We know that you can't come for them as you have no money for gas. You no longer have a cell phone, so there is no way for us to contact you in an emergency. You obviously are not comfortable telling us where you are going or what your plans are, probably because you don't have a plan. And it is not as if you normally call to check on your children regularly."

Surprisingly, Endora remained calm. I said nothing in a mean-spirited way, only in a matter-of-fact way. Endora never asked me why we took them to the hospital as opposed to calling the police or just calling DFS ourselves. I was thankful for that little reprieve, as I was not looking forward to tap dancing around the question. She did ask how the kids were doing and wanted to know if they asked for her. I told her that occasionally they did ask for her, and assured her that we never said anything bad about either her or Richie because we knew they loved her. She seemed to appreciate that. I told her that if she would contact Sandy and behave, that she and Richie would be allowed to call the kids and even visit them. But everything had to be approved through Sandy, and if Endora chose to scream and yell at her, she would only lessen the chances of DFS cooperating. Endora gave me her patented sarcastic laugh.

Later that evening Sandy called to say that she had spoken with Richie and Endora. She offered no details except that the conversation had not been pleasant. Still, as much as she hated the idea, she had to set up some parameters whereby the parents could speak to their kids, parameters that worked for us. She wanted to allow them two calls per week. We worked out the days, but I insisted on specifying the times. After I explained Endora's sleeping habits and described the last phone call she had made to the kids, Sandy agreed. So if Endora and/or Richie wanted to talk with the kids there were two days each week they could do so, and only between noon and 7:00 p.m. The calls were to last only fifteen minutes each. Also, she required Lucas and I to monitor every call by listening in on another phone. Endora and Richie had been made aware of this rule, and of the fact that DFS required it, not us. Sandy made it clear that we were to stick to this schedule, any change at all had to be approved by her. Endora and Richie would also be allowed to visit the kids, but the visits would be set up through her, take place at her office, and be supervised by her. Under no circumstances was either Endora or Richie allowed to come to our home. It was to be a safe space for the children. I can't stress enough that these were the rules put forth by DFS, not Lucas and Rene.

Chapter Thirty-two

Within the first week of having the kids, we learned that a court date had been set for the end of January. Endora and Richie needed to attend to present their cases, and we had no idea whether Richie would stick to his original story, that he brought us the kids with Endora's permission, or if he would show up and take Endora's side this time. We had a month until then to settle into a routine and all get used to each other.

The kids also had to get used to getting up each morning, taking care of their personal hygiene, having three meals a day, going to school (in Fancy Free's case), doing homework, being responsible for chores, having a bedtime and simply living normally with other people. They also needed to learn how to play outside with other children in the neighborhood: not to run out into the street, leave the house anytime they wanted, or walk into a neighbor's house without knocking and being invited in.

Oddly enough, the biggest change for me was feeling the need to prepare a meal every evening again. That meant going to the grocery store almost every day and actually spending the morning planning a well-balanced meal that everyone would enjoy that night. Lucas had always been so career-oriented that he rarely came home at dinnertime. When our children were little I could make nutritious meals that they would enjoy, but didn't have to worry if their dad would be pleased with the meal. As the girls got older and more involved with activities, we were all rarely home at dinnertime, and often ate fast-food dinners. Once Lucas began his early retirement and the kids started to drive, we would still eat out, but not always fast food. Now, we knew that nutrition, or the lack of it, was an issue for the kids, so instead of eating out five times a week we would eat at least five dinners a week at home. Joel and Fancy Free acted as if a feast had been set before them every evening, even if all I made was Hamburger Helper and a salad.

It didn't take long for our family to adjust, since we understood what was at stake. Joel and Fancy Free knew only one way of life. They were too young to understand that other people lived differently. I often wondered what they thought when they watched TV and saw people who didn't live in motels, sleep all day, go on the prowl at night, and live on candy bars and Coke. I guess they just thought that was how people lived on TV. But they didn't even seem to notice that we lived differently than Mom and Dad, other than the obvious differences that were forced on them from day one, like bedtimes. Or, at least, they didn't talk about it.

These kids' parents had set no boundaries. Even before their two years of living in motel rooms they had never had a bedtime. They just played or watched TV until they dropped off, and I suspect that was long after Dad went to sleep. Once they moved into the motels, they heard every adult conversation that took place, on the phone or in person. What must that alone have done to the kids? They heard their parents yelling and cussing at each other or other people. They heard their mother conning prospective employers, employers, schools, policemen, and anyone else she came across. Fancy Free may have been only six, but six was old enough to know if her mother was lying about why they were living at a motel, or why she had no medical records or hadn't been working. She knew it was a lie when she heard her mom tell the school that her daddy was a lawyer, while he was really driving a truck. She knew it was a lie when she heard her mom tell a landlord that she would pay him next week when she got her paycheck, a paycheck that didn't exist because she had no job. She knew it was a lie when Endora told a teacher that their house had burned down and they had lost everything.

In those motel rooms Joel and Fancy Free witnessed not only adult conversations, but also adult acts. Richie was gone a lot of the time, so I'm not sure what they saw happening between their parents sexually, but I know they saw acts of physical violence. Richie had told us of Endora's temper; she thought nothing of hauling off and hitting him or throwing something at him. He never mentioned his physical reaction, if any, but we know he came right back at her verbally. How? Anytime Joel got mad at Fancy Free he would call her "b——face."

And the children had definitely witnessed some sexual activity. Each morning, if Fancy Free woke up before I did, the first thing she would do was come into our bedroom, come over to me, and lift the sheet to see what I had on. If Lucas and I closed our bedroom door, she came unglued, and Nikki had to drag her back downstairs and tell her to leave us alone. She had no understanding of our right to be by ourselves.

One late afternoon, as I prepared dinner in the kitchen, Fancy Free came up to me and said, "Rene, what magazines does Lucas read?" I could tell by the look on her face that it was a loaded question. So I played stupid.

"I don't know, he gets several."

"Well, name them."

"*Golf Digest*."

"No."

"*In Fisherman*."

"No."

"*Newsweek*."

"No."

And so on, until I ran out of newspapers and magazines I knew Lucas read. By this time I'd figured out what she was getting at anyway, and just wanted to see if she would get to the point. "Fancy Free, he doesn't get any other magazines, so if you've seen anything else it must be mine." The look of shock on her face was priceless. "Fancy Free, have you been in my magazine basket in the bathroom?"

"Yes."

"Why don't you bring me what you were looking at?"

She said, "All right," and went to the bathroom to retrieve my latest *Victoria's Secrets* and *Venus Swimwear* catalogs. Of course, she'd focused only on the undergarments, obviously connecting them to pornography that she had seen Richie or some other man looking at. When I told her that I did most of my shopping through catalogs because I hated to shop, she remained unconvinced. So I said that if she turned past the first five or ten pages, she'd see that not only "those" things, but also lots of other clothes and things were sold in those magazines. She checked it out and became embarrassed. She knew she has revealed something that I probably should not know.

That evening all of my catalogs went into the trash.

Fancy Free felt as though it was her right to be in on everything that Lucas and I discussed. If we neglected to include her in the conversation, especially if a door was shut to keep her from hearing, it meant we were talking about her. On many occasions we sat her down and explained that most of our discussions concerned other things. She didn't grasp that we had three other daughters, parents, brothers and sisters, a home, and a whole host of other things to talk about. When we explained that children do not need to be a part of those conversations, she didn't understand why. After all, she could help us make decisions. She was baffled to hear that children weren't supposed to worry or make family decisions. That was what parents were for.

Fancy Free's kindergarten teacher ran into the same problems at school. Any time two adults were having a discussion, she needed to be listening in. When her teacher asked her to go back to work, she made a smart comment or got that "they must be talking about me" look on her face. It's not that she was paranoid. She truly felt that she should be in on the decision-making process. We told her that the only things six-year old girls should worry about were behaving in school, and "when do we eat?" That only made her laugh, but later it became an inside joke we shared with her. She would walk around saying over and over, "When do we eat?"

Not only did Fancy Free feel she should be making adult decisions, but she also acted as if she was Joel's mother. If we suspected that Joel had done something wrong, she covered for him and said that she did it. Then later she would discipline him. If we actually caught him in the act and started to talk with him about it, Fancy Free got very angry with us. We asked her to stay out of it, but then her smart mouth would kick in. The effect of this behavior: she could never just relax and be a kid. She doled out irrational punishments to Joel, the sort of verbal abuse she must have heard from her own mother. Since that had been her only training, she used it on Joel.

As for Joel, he lacked the ability to make a decision on his own. Fancy Free was too overbearing, just like her mother. Joel's loving nature made Endora's sick behavior penetrate his little mind even more effectively. Finally we had to sit Fancy Free down and tell her that Joel needed to make his own decisions. He would make mistakes, but that was the only way to learn and become independent. She looked at us as if we had two heads. Why would we want Joel to become independent? After all, he had her. We made a rule: she was not to tell on Joel or boss him around unless he was about to do something that could harm himself or someone else. If those situations arose, she had our permission to come to us. Under no circumstances was she to discipline him. At first this made her angry, but gradually we saw her understand that it took a lot of pressure off of her.

Fancy Free also lied constantly, just for the sake of lying. I could write a whole chapter just on the lies Endora had told us about herself. She would know that we knew she was lying, but she'd say it anyway. Like telling Maria and me that she had a job interview with the police department. Give me a break! Fancy Free had learned the same trick, and she could turn on the tears like turning on a faucet. Her acting made it hard for us to gauge just how traumatic things such as going to court really were for her. When real tears came, what if we thought they were just an act? We never knew for sure.

The biggest problem we encountered with Joel? Stealing. He had been taught to steal himself and to be the scapegoat in the event that Endora got caught. When Endora wanted to swipe something she would put it on Joel or in his pockets. Then, if she got caught, "My little boy must have grabbed that." In a checkout line with Joel we always had to keep one eye on him, otherwise he'd fill all of his pockets with whatever he saw. Then in the car or at home he would pull the stuff out. We always made him take it back and tell the store clerk or Sunday school teacher or whomever he had stolen from what he had done and that he was sorry. Only he was never sorry, or even upset that he had to do what we asked. He'd been doing it his whole life. He just stood there, looked you straight in the eyes, and said, "It's okay, I'm just a little boy."

Joel made meals an adventure, too. As the youngest and the littlest, he got the least to eat. But when he sat down to a meal he would stuff everything he could into his mouth at one time. He couldn't chew and would sometimes gag, but refused to spit anything out. It would take him ten minutes to finish chewing and to swallow. Nothing could ever be thrown out: if he had a McDonald's Happy Meal and didn't want all the fries, he would wrap them up and hide them in the refrigerator for later. If we told him they wouldn't taste any good later, it didn't matter. We had better not throw them away. He checked the next day to see if they were still there. Even when he knew he would never eat them because we had plenty of other food, he needed to know that those fries hadn't disappeared. He would share his toys, but not his food. Food was serious business.

By Joel's age, he should at least have been attempting to take care of certain issues of personal hygiene. Instead, he made me think of the scene in *Big Daddy* when Adam Sandler asks his new son, "Can you wipe your own a—?" These kids hadn't even been taught that much, which probably accounted for the fecal matter smeared on the walls at their original house. Joel would use the bathroom. Not wipe. Then walk around uncomfortably and start sticking his hand into the back of his pants, with the intent to pull out whatever he could and just wipe it wherever. I'm sure Endora had often left his diapers unchanged, and he'd gotten used to this behavior. Fortunately, one of us observed it early on and knew to watch for it. But it wasn't only Joel. Fancy Free never took the time for this ritual either. We never saw her attempt to clean herself the way her brother did, but her dirty laundry made it all too clear.

Because of their past and present issues at bath time, we tried to give the kids space in the bathroom on their own. So when they had to go, instead of going in with them we would remind them that they needed to wipe. This failed to work. Finally we had to tell them that the next time we found their underwear in the laundry in this condition, we would start assisting them in the bathroom until they proved that they would always take care of it themselves. Since Fancy Free had started to form friendships at school, her outgoing nature made it easy, though her bossiness would later get in the way. She often invited children over to play in the afternoons, and we had a little more leverage with her. She was not allowed to go over to someone else's house until she showed us that she would always attempt to clean herself.

The biggest problem for all of us was that these two kids had no sense of the needs of the rest of the world. Everything was about "I" or "me." They had no consideration for the other people living in the house with them. When they got up in the mornings, asking them to speak in lower voices so they wouldn't wake up other people just disgusted them. If more than one person wanted to watch TV, there was no discussing whose show won out. The idea of compromise had never been introduced to them.

Children of four and six are normally very self-centered, but this went way beyond that. We couldn't make them understand why it would hurt someone to steal from them, because every time they had gone on the run, all that they had was left behind. Why would lying hurt someone? Their whole world was a lie? Nothing existed beyond their own motel room; a constant "I want, I want, I want." It got so bad that Lucas finally made a rule: there would be no more "I want" in our house. That, too, became an inside joke. Joel and Fancy Free would walk around and take any opportunity to say, "That's an I want.'"

Chapter Thirty-two

The support that Neal and Maria gave to Lucas and I during the next six months cannot be measured. By Friday afternoon Lucas and I were always exhausted, and the weekends would have been equally fatiguing if it hadn't been for them. Our daughters' athletic activities filled the weekends, and getting Joel and Fancy Free out the door and to the games always made for a challenge. And their behavior once we got there left a lot to be desired. So we got into a routine of meeting Neal and Maria halfway between our homes on Friday evenings. They watched the kids through Sunday afternoon, when we would meet again so we could take them back for the week. Fancy Free had school Monday morning, and Neal and Maria had jobs to be at.

This routine also gave two other adults a chance to observe the kids' behavior, and provide invaluable information to the therapist that Fancy Free and Joel later had to see. It was quite a sacrifice for Neal and Maria, as they had to give up adult activities on the weekends. Hiring babysitters was out of the question for any of us. These two children were fearful of any new adult, or even teenager, who came into their lives. Lucas and I were so busy just keeping up with everyday family life that we often missed important signs that Neal and Maria picked up on.

For example, when Richie appeared at our home on Christmas Eve he had packed a grocery sack of clothes for each of the children. For some reason he had grabbed about fifteen pairs of panties for Fancy Free. I did laundry every day, so I didn't need that much underwear for her. Maria and I went through the clothes Richie left on Christmas Day, which wasn't much, and threw most of them away. They were either too small for the kids, who'd been raised on a diet of Coke and candy, too worn out, or too light for a Mid-West winter. During the first month we had them I often took them shopping for clothes, and if Maria had them she would do the same. Instead of having to pack for them every Friday and Sunday, we kept what they needed at each house. Since we had such a large supply of panties, I just sent half of them to Maria's. Thankfully Maria took the time to look more thoroughly at them than I did.

So far, we had found reason to be suspicious of inappropriate sexual activity, the kids' behavior at bath times and diaper changes, Fancy Free's drawings in Endora's journals, her questions regarding my catalogs and need to look under our covers each morning. But we had no physical evidence until Maria uncovered the most telling of clues, within a week of Sandy approving her help on the weekends: Maria discovered panties with large bloodstains.

The discovery sickened us. Up to that point we could at least pray that all the other clues pointed to some other reason for their strange behavior. Now we knew someone had done something unspeakable to Fancy Free. We showed the underwear to Sandy and, shortly thereafter, a psychiatrist who was assigned to Fancy Free for evaluation. They believed that we were looking at bloodstains. Those panties have never left our possession. We figured with that kind of evidence, surely no judge would send the kids back to either parent until one of them confessed.

At that point, DFS and Fancy Free's doctors decided that maybe we should not do the SAMs test on her. Apparently, most molestation does not involve the actual insertion of the penis, and in this case there could be enough irritation in the vaginal area to cause bleeding but not enough to damage the hymen. If this was the case, the results of the test could be used against us in court. Therefore everyone agreed to let the evidence we already had speak for itself. And not subject Fancy Free to further humiliation.

In the end, it didn't matter. We would never get to present our evidence to the judge anyway.

Chapter Thirty-three

At the end of January Richie called again. He'd decided that it was all a lost cause, and wanted to come back home to Missouri. He wanted Lucas to send him money for bus fare, an easy decision this time. Lucas informed Richie that not only would he not be receiving any money, he was also unwelcome at our home if he did find a way to get back to Missouri. He was allowed contact with the kids only at Sandy's office; so living with us was no longer an option. Several days later he called from the downtown bus station. Lucas went there to pick up his brother, a former Colonel in the Air Force and prosecuting attorney, to take him to a city homeless shelter.

We let all of Lucas's siblings know what had happened and where Richie was living. Richie would likely contact one of them for help and shelter, and we wanted to let them know that we wouldn't blame them for saying yes but that we had come to the conclusion that saying yes to Richie generally led to hurt for the children. At this point in the game our focus was 100 percent on Joel and Fancy Free, and we hoped that no one would interpret that as callousness toward Richie. If they chose to help Richie, we wouldn't view it as a betrayal of us. We didn't want the family to split up and take sides, but we did want them to be aware that any action they took to help Richie could affect the well being of his children. We have kept the knowledge of Fancy Free's sexual abuse from them to this day.

Everyone in the family gathered up warm clothing for Richie. Neal and Maria even drove into town with some coats. After delivering the items, Lucas's sisters decided they couldn't stand to see Richie live this way. So Nancy invited him to live with her and her husband in their home until he got a job. That situation didn't last long, Richie was more like another child than a houseguest, and Nancy lacked the patience to put up with him. Richie soon found himself back in the shelter. He did find a job as a night shift security officer at the airport. He would try to get some sleep during the daytime, and when he was awake he'd be working toward getting his law license reinstated. The license had to be renewed each year, and attendance at certain classes was required to keep it current. During the past couple of years Richie had let it lapse, and now he had to work to have any chance of getting his career back.

But who would ever hire him as an attorney? Hindsight may be 20/20, but we saw that problem coming from the beginning. Still, he was trying to reignite his career and we had to give him credit. It would cost money that Richie didn't have, but Lucas stood firm and refused to help him. So Richie worked all night, spent several hours a day at the public library, and attended the necessary classes. The little bit of money he made had to be budgeted carefully.

Endora's whereabouts remained a mystery. She did call

the kids regularly at first, but knew that we were listening in on their conversations, so her comments to them were vague. She always had a grand story of the new job she was starting soon as a doctor, and of the house they all would live in. The children loved their mom and her tales. They preferred the reality of our home, but they still wanted the storybook ending with Mom.

It broke our hearts to see them get off the phone with renewed hope. And then we had to deal with the belief that Mom was coming soon, and their current life was only temporary. The attitude that they were just guests and that our life was not real life would emerge for about twenty-four hours, and then we'd get back on track. Still, we refused to tell the kids that their mother was lying to them. After several months of phone calls from their mother in which she described her plans for the future that never came, the children created their own best-case scenario: life would be perfect if they could go on living with us forever, with Mom in a tent in the backyard. When they voiced these feelings, we realized they were starting to enjoy normal family life and to fear returning to their old life. But despite those fears, they still wanted their mom to be in their lives. Not to take care of them, but to love them.

Chapter Thirty-four

The hearing to determine whether DFS would gain custody was set for February 10th. As we approached the date, Endora still lacked a job, so we doubted she would show. What would be the point? She feared entering the state of Missouri, which had all kinds of outstanding warrants out for her. Without a job or decent place to live, what chance did she have to regain custody anyway? Sandy called to tell us that Endora asked for the case to be continued to a later date; it was now to take place on March 7th. We felt pretty positive: how could Endora walk into a courtroom in March and claim that her children had been kidnapped in December?

Unfortunately, the postponement gave Endora time to find another hospital willing to give her a job. In February, she told Sandy that she had gotten work at a hospital in Selma, Alabama. Sandy's attempts to verify that claim turned out to be untrue. Shortly thereafter, however, Endora reported finding a job as a physician at Pickens County Hospital in Pickens County, Alabama. Again, Sandy called the hospital and was told that Endora didn't work there. But it turned out that Endora was indeed working there; the hospital simply refused to verify it to anyone. Endora must have pulled something fishy to get the job, otherwise why would a hospital administrator lie about it to DFS? She may have been a terrible parent, but she was a skilled con artist.

Not only did Pickens County hire Endora, but, according to Endora, they also provided benefits such as a house to live in, money to help purchase a car and to hire an attorney for the custody battle, and time off to come to Missouri for the hearings and visitations. I can't even begin to imagine the tale she must have spun to get those people to do all of that for her. It's safe to say that Pickens County Hospital was hurting for physicians.

Now we faced a real battle. Our experience with the court system had taught us that it was all about the parents, especially the mother, and reuniting the family. No one would do their homework and gather all of Endora's history from Birmingham and Huntsville. So did we sit and take our chances that the system would actually work for the kids this time, or did we take action? Endora had left Missouri with a string of warrants, along with numerous unpaid vehicle violations. She also had rented a car in the state of Illinois without honoring her contract, the rental agency, like so many other businesses, had contacted us hoping to get their money. She had illegally removed a tracking device they put on their cars so that when something like this happened, they could find and retrieve the car. One would think that keeping the car for nine months would be considered car theft, but perhaps the agency preferred to just get the car back without having to pay the attorney's fees required to go to court. Our dilemma: Should we try to use any of that information to help the kids?

We never wanted to hurt Endora, but the system forced us to consider it. We knew they would likely give the kids back to Endora unless she actually ended up in jail. As Lucas and I were discussing which avenue to take, we got another call from the car rental agency. Lucas explained that we knew how they could get their car back, but if they wanted our help they needed to file charges. Why they hadn't done so before, we had no idea. Once they got the car back, they couldn't accuse her of theft, but they could file charges for removing the tracking device. They promised to go to the police and file every charge possible: she had breached their contract, owed them a lot of money, kept their car for nine months, trashed it, and removed the device. In return, we told them the date Endora had to be in court and the location of the courthouse. We even agreed to wait until she arrived and then place a call to the company so they wouldn't waste their time coming to get the car if she hadn't shown up. In the end, the car rental company reneged on their end of the deal. They got their car and never filed any report.

Still wary of where he stood, we told Richie about none of this. He'd returned to Missouri in the middle of January. The first attempt to contact the kids occurred on February 27th. He called Sandy to set up a visitation at her office the following day. Everyone, including Sandy, knew that it was all for show. We were due in court seven days later, so if Richie expected the judge to show any respect for him as a parent, he'd better have visited his children at least once by then.

The morning of March 7th, our home was filled with

tears; we had to tell Joel and Fancy Free about the situation since they were required to come with us in case the judge took custody from DFS and forced us to return the kids to their mother. We waited until that morning, as telling them ahead of time would only cause anxiety to build. Fancy Free burst into tears, believing we were telling her that she had to go back to Mom. Joel was confused; every time they talked to Endora, Fancy Free liked to mess with his mind and tell him they were going back. Despite our scolding, she would whisper it to him at bedtime, we heard, of course, since she had no sense of what it was to whisper. Upsetting him gave her power over him, the same kind of treatment she had always gotten from her mom. Afterward, she could act as if going back to Endora was a good thing and console him. Now, Fancy Free thought the time of reckoning had arrived. Joel, on the other hand, couldn't understand her tears: she'd been telling him for a month how good going back would be.

We tried to use this moment to teach Fancy Free why she should not have said such things to her brother. We knew she had no desire to return to their old way of life, so why choose to torture Joel that way? It was okay to love her mother and want to live with us at the same time. We assured her that we would do everything possible to keep things from changing. She was upset with us for not sharing the truth with her sooner. We again explained that worrying was our job, not hers, and reminded her that her job consisted of going to school and doing her homework. The rest was for the adults to worry about. The conversation calmed her down, but only a little.

Neal and Maria drove in and met us at the courthouse. Once inside, we found out that they would not be allowed up to the floor that the courtroom is on. The proceedings had changed now that DFS had custody of the children. Joel and Fancy Free had never officially been placed with Neal and Maria, so the hearing would go on without them. Once Lucas and I had checked in, we saw Sandy, Richie, and his attorney. The hearing would begin in ten minutes. Where was Endora?

The hour arrived, and we all entered. The parties involved included Sandy and the attorney for DFS, Richie and his attorney, the court-appointed attorney representing the children (no longer Gale Shoffler), Lucas and I, and another attorney who represented Endora, but no Endora. We could tell that Mr. Swift, Endora's attorney, was a bit agitated. Welcome to the party. Judge Metcalf entered the courtroom and all parties were introduced. Still, no Endora. Lucas and I looked at each other and Lucas whispered, "This is really getting good." As Endora's attorney explained to the judge that she might have been delayed because she had to pay some past vehicle violation citations before appearing, Endora walked in, panicked.

She sat next to her attorney and began talking to him as though no one else was there. Jittery and agitated, she showed obvious signs of needing medication. We all looked at her and then at the judge to see what her reaction would be. The judge remained poker-faced, but it was evident that every other person in the courtroom now understood what we had been dealing with. The judge began again, asking the attorney for DFS to state the basic case against the parents. As the attorney began to explain that their father had brought the children to Missouri, Endora started her interruptions. The judge asked her to be quiet, but a few minutes later she piped up again. The third interruption was the last straw.

"Mrs. Howitt, I understand that you are a doctor."

"Yes."

"I don't believe I would enter your operating room and tell you how to conduct your business, so you will not be allowed to speak in my courtroom until I have addressed you. Is that clear?"

"Yes, I'm just very upset."

"I can see that. If you will give me a moment, perhaps I can better understand why."

In the next few minutes Judge Metcalf heard the details of how we had all gotten there that day. Then Endora's attorney, Mr. Swift, whom Lucas would later nickname "Not To," began to state their case, he believed that the state of Missouri had no jurisdiction over the matter. Mr. Swift spoke for only a few minutes before the judge ruled that more investigation was needed before a ruling on the jurisdiction matter. All parties pulled out their planners and worked on finding a date for the next court proceeding, at which time the judge would decide whether the state of Missouri did in fact have the right to take custody of the children. I couldn't believe what I was watching. The judge threw out the first date that worked for her. If one of the attorneys had a prior commitment, the judge threw out another date. This continued until all parties agreed on one date and time, after at least five suggested dates and times from the judge.

That was it for the day, after no more than fifteen minutes and not one question about the welfare or condition of the children. We would all return in April, when the children might be returned to the state of Alabama. Then Alabama would have custody and would need to determine whether the children should be returned to their mother.

I'm not the most educated person in the world, but it seemed to me that we had just wasted a lot of the state's time and money on a judge, an attorney for DFS, an attorney to represent Richie (he couldn't afford one), a Guardian Ad Litem to represent the children (who had never even met them), and court expenses to meet and decide to: *What, meet again?* Perhaps there would be more money for social services in this country if we actually accomplished something with it. Shouldn't the judge at least have taken the time to find out why DFS saw reason to intervene? What if they'd made a mistake and taken the children unjustly from their mother? She now had to wait another month for her day in court. If DFS did have a substantial case against the mother, shouldn't the state spend its time and money during the next month determining whom in Alabama would work on the case if it did have to go back there?

But the next hearing would determine only which state had jurisdiction. Even if the case remained in Missouri, no time had been slotted to hear evidence. We would have to meet again in May for that purpose. If jurisdiction were shifted to Alabama, would anyone be prepared to handle it? Would the court hand the children to their mother and say, "Let Alabama worry about this?" Or would the state of Missouri contact officials in Alabama to set up a transfer? In either scenario, would anyone have thought about the effect on Joel and Fancy Free?

Scenario one: the children go from us to Endora, who then takes them on the run. Scenario two: they go from us to DFS, who then transfers them to DHR in Alabama, who then places them in a foster family they've never met. All after we have spent over two months helping them adjust to a new life, establishing Fancy Free in school, and, most important, teaching them to bond with a real family.

When Endora finally made her appearance, Lucas slipped out into the hallway and made the call to the car rental agent, who was waiting in the area just in case things worked out. When Lucas verified that Endora was there, they knew their car was in the parking lot. So at the hearing's end, Endora's means of transportation had vanished. I don't know how Endora got back to Alabama, but the following day her attorney had to drive her to the DFS office for a visitation with the kids.

On that day, March 8th, we had to have the kids at the DFS office by noon so they could see their mom. Joel's fourth birthday had passed on February 10, and neither Mom nor Dad had acknowledged it. We figured the same thing had happened to Fancy Free on her birthday in December, so along with Neal and Maria we had planned a big party for them both on Joel's birthday. Now, Endora had apparently decided to make up for all her mistakes in one day. When the kids emerged from the visitation they had more junk and junk food than I could have imagined. Sandy looked both exhausted and disgusted, and the kids had food all over their hair, hands, and clothes. We had to make several trips to load everything into my car.

When we got home and started sorting through all of the stuff, I couldn't believe my eyes. It was as though every time Endora walked into a store she had grabbed every crappy little toy she saw. The kinds of toys that stores keep right by the checkout counters so your kids will beg you for them while you stand in line. Then, by the time you get home, they're already broken. Sandy had warned us that these kinds of parents do exactly that: try to make up for all of their wrongs in one visit. Adults saw through it, but kids didn't. Suddenly Endora was the greatest mom in the world, and they had forgotten about being left alone and hungry, getting knocked around, and all the rest. After one two-hour visit, their behavior regressed to what it had been two months earlier. They no longer listened to us, and became hyperactive. Each visit with Endora, which usually occurred when she was in town for a hearing, resulted in at least two days like that. As for Richie, he only visited them once.

Chapter Thirty-five

Endora returned to Pickens County to work at the hospital. She set up one more visitation with the children prior to the next court date on March 26. Since Alabama was a good ten-hour drive from Missouri, her doing so actually impressed me; Richie didn't call or try to see the kids more than once or twice in the six months we had them.

Both Endora and Richie had the right to call our house two times per week, between 12:00 and 7:00 on Wednesday and Sunday, to speak with the kids. We made every effort to keep the kids home during those times. When spring came and that wasn't always possible because of other activities, we always let the kids call Endora back as soon as we got home with them. Sandy always found out from us if we had caused the delay, though most times we told Endora in advance about any conflict. Richie never called, so we knew where his kids stood on his priority list. And although Endora called, most of the time she waited until the last minute and called ten to fifteen minutes late. Sandy had told Lucas and me to strictly adhere to the rules, but we knew it was a game to Endora, a way to show control. Not letting her speak to the kids seemed unfair to them, so we would act as if we didn't notice she had called late. The kids didn't know, so why make an issue over ten minutes? Unfortunately, giving Endora an inch only made her push harder. Some nights her call would come an hour or two late, and we just wouldn't answer the phone. As time passed, she began to not call at all on the specified days, or call only once a week. She blamed it on her job. Apparently she couldn't take a fifteen-minute lunch break to call her kids. Luckily, most of those times Joel and Fancy Free didn't even notice or ask about her. If she didn't call life went much more smoothly for us.

Endora had a problem with two issues regarding the phone: we had to listen in, and we got to control the topics of conversation. It wasn't necessary for the kids to know in advance about court dates, but Sandy had anticipated that Endora would try to use her calls to discuss such matters with the children. Unlike most mature adults, she didn't understand that conversations of that nature would only scare the children and cause them unnecessary stress, in turn causing behavior and sleep problems. We tried to explain to Endora that the kids should know that we were all going to court occasionally in order to work out what was best for them. She wanted them to think it was Lucas and Rene against her. That's when we had to end the conversation.

She would tell the kids about her new house, and how she was decorating their rooms with new furniture, paint, and all new toys. She filled their heads with the things children dream of. And they got off the phone with attitudes. Fancy Free liked to remind us that we were not her mom.

A couple of weeks later, when Endora set up another

visitation, Fancy Free was in morning kindergarten, which got out at 11:30. I picked her up so we would have time to feed her and Joel lunch before their noon meeting with Mom. Lucas and I had also set aside any other activities that afternoon to get the kids there and be available to pick them up after the visitation. As soon as I picked Fancy Free up, I told them they were going to see their mom that day, filling them with excitement.

When we arrived at the DFS office I saw Sandy but Endora hadn't gotten there yet. Twenty minutes passed, still no Endora. Sandy tried to contact her by phone with no luck. Angry at having wasted half an hour of her day, Sandy told me to take the kids home. As soon as the kids and I walked in the door the phone was ringing, it was Sandy calling to say Endora would be at her office at 2:00. She gave me the option of refusing to bring the kids back but I declined because, again, I felt it would only be punishing the kids. Sandy suggested that I wait at home and she would call me when and if Endora actually arrived. Good idea: 2:00 arrived, but Endora didn't. Finally, at 3:30, Endora showed up at the DFS office. Sandy let her have it, telling her that she would not require me to bring the kids there unless I wanted to, and that on any future visits if Endora was even five minutes late she would forfeit the visit entirely. I did take the children to see their mom, but only because I had gotten their hopes up earlier in the day. After the visit I regretted allowing it because I had to deal with all the junk and bad attitudes again. Endora had ruined yet another day.

Chapter Thirty-six

Richie mentioned to us before the first hearing that Endora had hired an attorney in Alabama, so Mr. Swift's presence had surprised us (he resided in Missouri). Someone must have suggested to Endora that she find an attorney licensed in the state of Missouri. But she did retain an attorney in Alabama as well, if jurisdiction was transferred there, Mr. Swift would be of no use to her. She was covering all the angles.

Several days before the next hearing, a reliable source in Alabama told us that Endora had not only retained another attorney, but was also living with him. This source warned us that her new attorney, Mr. Thorton Wainscoat, had a checkered background and that we had better do some checking up on him. The source told us nothing else, except that doing the research shouldn't be hard.

During the course of this saga, two different sources that we cannot identify fed us information, and this was one of them. In this case a career was put on the line for the sake of the children. The motivation: as bad as things had been for the children in the past, if the accusations against this new attorney were true and Endora got custody back, Joel and Fancy Free's quality of life would hit an all-time low.

Neal got busy on the Internet going through back issues of the Alabama newspapers, looking for any article that mentioned a Thorton Wainscoat. But the first thing he came across didn't mention Wainscoat. It was the following notice from the February 19, 2003, edition, in the Police Reports Arrest section:

> Endora Terry Howitt, 42, of 4040 Citation Road, was charged with possession of a controlled substance. Bail was set at $1000.00.

Endora had asked the court for a continuance for the February 10th hearing so that she could be better prepared to fight for her children in March. Meanwhile, she was getting arrested on drug charges.

It gets better. When we asked Richie if he was aware of the arrest, he said no, but it didn't surprise him. He said that while he was with Endora in Alabama, prior to bringing the children to us at Christmas, he had discovered several bottles of prescription narcotics with Fancy Free's and Joel's names on them. Doctors can't prescribe medicines for themselves, so Endora wrote prescriptions for her children. And she was likely not just taking the drugs, but turning around and selling them, too. We asked Richie to do the right thing and report it to the Alabama State Board of Medical Examiners and he actually did so. This probably led to Endora's second loss of her medical license. Why didn't Richie report it when he first found out? Who knows?

Neal continued searching for information on Mr. Wainscoat, and found the next astounding newsflash: articles dated September 26, November 1, and December 3, 2002, regarding Pickens County Judge Thorton Wainscoat.

In a complaint filed by the Judiciary Inquiry Commission on August 6th, Wainscoat was accused of having inappropriate physical contact with seven females between 1998 and 2002. In several of the allegations, Wainscoat had been accused of touching women's breasts while hugging them.

The Alabama Court of the Judiciary had suspended Wainscoat for six months in October 1994 for violating four judicial canons of ethics involving personal conduct. He was accused of touching several teenage girls and adult women on their breasts, thighs, stomachs, or buttocks during meetings in his office or in public.

In one of the allegations in the August 2002 complaint, Wainscoat was said to have told a young girl to walk behind the bench and stand next to him during the hearing. The complaint alleges that Wainscoat placed his arms around her and pulled her close, holding her that way for fifteen minutes while speaking to her. Wainscoat kissed the girl, described as between eight and ten years old, on the cheek after he finished speaking, according to the complaint.

Wainscoat resigned rather than stand trial on these accusations of improper contact with females who had cases heard in his court. Under an agreement with the Judiciary Inquiry Commission, Wainscoat had turned in a letter of resignation and the charges against him were dismissed.

So the judge resigned to avoid being disbarred and losing his pension, but he could still practice law. Endora not only hired him but let him move in with her. Now she wanted her four-and six-year old children to live with this man, too. We thought this was just more evidence we could provide to DFS and to Judge Metcalf, displaying Endora' lack of judgement.

Chapter Thirty-seven

On March 26, 2003, we went to court to find out about the case's jurisdiction. The Guardian Ad Litem still had not met the children. We had hired an attorney who was greatly respected by the court in hopes of having a voice this time. We wanted Judge Metcalf to be aware of at least a few of our fears that were unrelated to the jurisdiction issues. We still had trouble believing that our judicial system was such that anything at all would take priority over the safety and welfare of a child. Our attorney advised us that he didn't believe, even with him there, that our voice would be heard. We hired him anyway.

Endora actually arrived on time. We sat in the courtroom for only a short time before being asked to step outside. Only the attorneys and the judge remained. Lucas and Richie wandered off down the hall, leaving Endora and I to sit on separate benches maybe twenty feet from each other. She started to fidget and then pace. Finally she confronted me.

"Why do you want my children?"

I just look at her and said, "Endora, someone has to take care of them."

"But they're mine."

"They're human beings who need to be taken care

of. Saying you love them is not enough." Oddly, she just walked away. The conversation could have been a lot worse.

Endora was then led back into the courtroom, where the police were waiting, to arrest her for some of those bad checks. Finally, some justice, though it wouldn't last long, she got out of jail in fewer than twenty-four hours. Again, the judge had heard not one word of testimony regarding the children. The parties had agreed that jurisdiction belonged in Alabama, so now the kids were Endora's. But when Endora was arrested and taken into custody, DFS could step back in since Endora couldn't care for them while in jail, and there would have to be another hearing no matter how long she spent there. DFS then placed them back with us, and a new hearing date was set for April 10th.

This time, two issues had been settled: jurisdiction went to Alabama, and Endora got arrested. Then we were done for the day. No opportunity, with everyone gathered, to discuss the real issue. Under current law, as soon as the judge decided that jurisdiction belonged in Alabama, she was done. It was no longer her responsibility, even though the kids remained in Missouri and in the custody of DFS. Just move on to the next case.

While everyone pranced around congratulating themselves on their solution to protect the kids, Lucas was telling them how wrong they were. Their solution was nothing but a Band-Aid. Eventually it would come off. Everyone thought it was great that Endora was now in jail, but for some reason they decided that jurisdiction belonged in Alabama. Since we were not in the courtroom for that part, I still don't know why. As soon as Endora got out of jail, she would be legally entitled to have her kids back. She wouldn't get them until the next court date, but she had essentially won the fight. The only tactic we could use we borrowed from Endora: asking for continuances. We did manage to get the case postponed until May 16, 2003. Our only hope was that Endora would get herself into enough trouble between March 26 and May 16 that she would end up back in jail and unable to come back for Joel and Fancy Free.

Chapter Thirty-eight

But Endora managed to stay out of trouble until May 16. Lucas and I knew it spelled the end for the kids. Fancy Free was about two weeks shy of finishing kindergarten, but that wouldn't matter to Endora. She probably wouldn't even let Fancy Free say good-bye to her new friends.

Our daughter Nikki stayed home from school with the children, for some reason DFS didn't ask us to bring them to court this time. The kids knew where we were going, but we didn't tell them it would probably be the last time. We let Fancy Free stay home from school on that Friday, afraid that as soon as Endora regained custody she would go to the school and drag her daughter out of class. The disruption it would cause the teacher and the rest of the class wouldn't matter, nor would the anger, embarrassment, and confusion for Fancy Free.

We all gathered in the courtroom for this final session. It looked as though the judge was finally going to hear some evidence. The attorney for DFS once again presented a brief explanation of why we came to have the kids. Then Endora's attorney, Mr. Swift was allowed to question her about how all this came about. She made sure to use the word kidnapping as often as possible, but had a hard time just answering the questions and staying on the subject at hand. The judge had to remind her several times to stick to the questions asked. Richie's attorney asked her a few questions. Our attorney and the guardian passed on the opportunity to hear her rant any further.

Now it appeared to be Richie's turn, the moment of truth for him. The little faith we had in Richie had faded even more since his return to Missouri. He showed very little interest in his children and spent no energy preparing for what we felt would inevitably happen that day. Before Richie took the stand, Lucas and I were inexplicably asked to leave the courtroom. Afterward, our attorney told us that before Richie gave testimony, Judge Metcalf decided to rule that DFS no longer had custody of the children. That way, it would be Alabama's problem. One side had been allowed to speak, but not the other. Richie didn't even seem upset in the courtroom; it was almost as if it had all been set up ahead of time.

Outside, Richie tried to put on a show, like he believed the situation was unfair. He even agreed to move out of his current living quarters and back into our home for the weekend. Lucas asked his brother to do that, because even though DFS had to give up custody, no one has actually told us that we had to turn the kids back over to Endora. So if Richie moved back into our house, we'd be back where we were on Christmas Eve. Since Joel was his son, he had as much right to him as Endora did, at least until a judge said otherwise. If Richie wasn't living with us, when Endora showed up with the police we would have no choice but to turn the children over to her. We tried to convince Richie to get a Protective Order of Custody filed that day on Joel, as he had done the previous year. He said he would make some calls when we got home.

When we got home Lucas and I took the kids upstairs to our bedroom so we could talk to them without Richie listening in. He was supposed to be making an attempt to contact his attorney and hopefully get an Order of Protection filed for Joel. Time was of the essence; it was now Friday afternoon. We knew that we could hold off the police over the weekend, but come Monday, Endora would go before a judge if she had to.

Telling Fancy Free and Joel that they had to go back to their mom was the hardest thing Lucas and I have ever had to do. After six months, the kids had made friends and become a part of a real family. Even though Fancy Free still talked with Joel about how great going home to Mom would be someday, they really dreamed of staying with us, with Mom in that tent in the backyard. When we told them of the judge's decision, Fancy Free went to pieces. She'd seen enough and was smart enough to understand that this time it was over. She cried and shook and clung to Lucas, which was very unusual, she always came to me for physical attention. Somehow she thought that Lucas was her only chance to stay, but this time even Lucas didn't have the answers. He just held her and cried with her. Joel just stood right behind Fancy Free, rubbing her back and consoling her, telling her how much he loved her and that everything would be all right. I think deep down Fancy Free always knew they would have to go back, so she had been preparing Joel all along. But nothing had prepared her.

Things played out just as we suspected. Richie failed to get a hold of his attorney, and the police showed up Friday evening with Endora. We didn't answer the door. They left, only to return later that night, late enough that Lucas and I were the only ones still awake. The lights were all off and Lucas and I lay in bed watching TV. We heard the cars pull up out front. Staying out of sight, we watched them gather in the street, the police, Endora, and her attorney. Once again we just ignored the knocking. The police remained fairly quiet, so we knew they were only there to appease Endora.

On Saturday night when we again didn't answer the door, the police called us. They asked Lucas if he would at least come out and talk with them. Lucas told them what happened in court and that we had not been told to turn the children over to Endora, only that DFS no longer had custody. Since the father was living with us, we planned to keep the children until Endora got a court order saying we had to turn them over. The police asked to see Richie. Once they verified his presence, they told Endora she would have to get the court order.

Monday morning, May 19th we knew this was it. We packed the kids in our van with a few toys. Richie was going to take them to his attorney's office. We knew he would do nothing to stop Endora, and that this was the last we would see Joel and Fancy Free.

Richie, the big bad prosecuting attorney, had let his wife beat him at his own game. On Friday afternoon her attorney had prepared an Order of Protection for Joel, exactly what Lucas had told Richie to have his attorney prepare. She went before a judge on Monday morning and got it signed. Richie never had any right to Fancy Free, so we were finished.

Lucas and Richie's sister Liz met Richie to help him with the transfer of the children. He said his good-byes to them at his attorney's office and had Liz deliver them to Endora in a park, probably a smart move, as it avoided a confrontation. Maria and Neal never had a chance to say good-bye.

Lucas and I deliberately went our separate ways that day while our kids were in school. We each needed to process the loss in our own way. Later in the day when we got home, Richie had been there and returned our van. Liz had brought Richie to our home to return the van and pick up his things. Lucas had already told Richie that once he stopped fighting for Joel we didn't want him around anymore. Richie moved in with Liz and her husband, Tim, that day. Neither of us has talked to him since.

The answering machine light was blinking. Lucas and I stood in the kitchen, sort of waiting for our girls to come home from school. Lucas pushed the button and we heard Fancy Free's voice. She was weeping. Her mother had made her call us, sort of a "Ha ha!" call. We heard Endora in the background, telling her what to say.

Chapter Thirty-nine

Shortly after Endora left for Pickens County, I sat down and drafted a letter to the Pickens County Hospital Administrator, explaining that I wished Endora well and that if she were doing well and seemed healthy, they could disregard my letter. However, if they ever needed to let Endora go or felt suspicious about any of her activities, they should please consider the children. The bottom line was that if they had any doubts about anything, they should contact DHR. An inquiry suggested by them would mean a lot more than one suggested by me. We found out a short time later that Endora never returned to work at Pickens County Hospital. She had gotten them to give her a job, a house, a car, lawyer's fees, and time to fight for her kids. What had she given them in return?

When I got this information I contacted the local DHR office in Pickens County. I gave them Endora's address and told the caseworker of her history in Huntsville, Missouri, and Birmingham. I explained that Endora would run in the middle of the night if she felt threatened in any way, that she had a history of this and, as a doctor, she knew the system very well. I also explained that Endora could con anyone. Her response: "Ms. Howitt, I used to be a juvenile officer. There isn't anyone who can con me."

When I explained the con that Endora had just pulled on a hospital administrator and asked her to call the hospital to verify, she was skeptical. She treated me like every other caseworker I had talked with in Missouri and Alabama, with the exception of Sandy. At that point we could only leave the situation in God's hands, as we had done so many months before.

I returned home one evening that September to find a phone message from a woman in Alabama. She wanted to know if we had any connection to Joel Howitt and Fancy Free, and if so, could we please call her. Of course, I called immediately. It turned out she lived on the same street as Endora and the kids.

She told me that in the six months they had lived there, she had never once seen the kids' mother outside. They ran all over with no supervision. They came up to her house for food. The new school year had started, and Fancy Free was not going. The final straw: two evenings ago, her husband came home from work at midnight and found the two kids playing in the middle of the street. No one was watching them. Finally, she'd gotten our names from the kids and Googled us to find our phone number. I asked her to call DHR. She said that she already had. This was their response: "Does the house the children live in have blinds on the windows?" The neighbor's response: "Why yes, it does." DHR: "Then how do you know that the mother isn't sitting inside watching the children play through the blinds?" They are four and six years old playing in the street at mid night!

I asked the neighbor if she would contact the school

and let them know that she had tracked us down. Explain that we had been the kids' foster parents, that there were unresolved cases in Alabama and Missouri, and that this child should be in first grade. The neighbor did all of this, and a truant officer did see that Fancy Free was enrolled in school. At least someone took action.

One of our sources informed us that the Alabama State Board of Medical Examiners showed up at Endora's front door. While they were inside informing her that they were taking away her license to practice medicine again, the caseworker from DHR showed up to start her investigation. Endora had to ask her to wait outside until she finished with the State Examiner.

In October, the neighbor called again to say that Endora and the kids had disappeared in the middle of the night. She was on the run again, exactly what we had told the caseworker would happen back in June.

Back in May, Richie had moved in with Tim and Liz. It took him a while, but he finally got a job at a gas-station convenience store. He tried for months to get a job working as an attorney; he had managed to get his license reinstated. But he found it hard to get a job as an attorney when he had to explain the last four years away and he was almost sixty years old. He couldn't just say, "I don't want to talk about it." Surely if he told them the truth and any follow-up was done regarding past employment, they wouldn't find any glowing recommendations.

Richie eventually gave up on being a lawyer, but did get promoted into management at his convenience-store job. He lived with Tim and Liz for about six months and then moved into a one-room apartment. He couldn't afford much, as his first wife, Natasha, had tracked him down and was hounding him for back child support. We know Endora called for money, too, even though at some point during the past couple of years she and Richie were finally divorced, and he gave up all rights to Joel.

Once in a while Maria would call Richie just to see if he had talked with the kids recently. He was always very vague because he knew Maria would give us any leads she could get. It was always the same story: "The kids are doing just great." Then he told her in May 2004 that Endora had landed another job in Nashville, Tennessee. This time she was working for a doctor, doing research at a very large hospital. The doctor had an unusual name, so my brother-in-law, Neal, went to work searching the hospital website and found his phone number. Maria called his office and asked to speak to Endora. She was told that Endora wasn't in, so we knew the job was for real.

We tried everything we could to get Endora's new address, but never found any record. Endora knew better than to get a land phone line. She only used cell phones. We desperately wanted her address so we could narrow down the number of schools the children could attend that September. Joel should have been starting kindergarten and Fancy Free second grade. If we could narrow it to a neighborhood, we planned to send letters to all the area grade schools. If we happened to hit the one they were attending, at least they would know to report any unusual behavior right away.

By October 2004, Endora had lost her job and disappeared again. This time we had no details about what happened with her job or the school the kids had been enrolled in. We totally lost track of the children and could do nothing but pray.

Chapter Forty

Seven months later, in May 2005, Endora surfaced again. We got a tip that social services in Alabama might be involved again. When we could not confirm this on our own, Lucas sent an email to the governor, the lieutenant governor, and the head of DHR in Alabama. He explained our history with the children as well as the established cases in Birmingham and Pickens County, not to mention Missouri. Lucas sent the e-mail on a Friday afternoon. On Monday morning we got a phone call from Carla, who worked for the head of DHR. Lucas asked her to look into the situation immediately. She told us that the kids were in foster care in Alabama and that the caseworker would contact us within two weeks. Two days later, Dixie, the new caseworker assigned in Anniston, called us.

Endora had been arrested and was serving a six-month sentence for fourteen counts of writing bad checks in Birmingham. The children had been placed in voluntary foster care. Endora gave the state a false statement that no family was available to care for the children. She also lied about the reason the kids needed temporary housing, her incarceration, and when they finally found out, it took them two weeks to determine which jail Endora was in and for how long. In fact, my brother-in-law Neal was able to locate this information online before the state did. At some point Richie was contacted by social services, they would have wanted to know if he was in a position to care for the children. He obviously indicated that he wasn't. Regardless of what other lies Endora concocted to get the state to agree to foster care, and regardless of whether Richie went along with those lies, we know one thing: he never mentioned that he had a brother and a sister who would take in the children. Instead both he and Endora opted to have their children placed in foster care with strangers.

On May 25th, Lucas received a call from Dixie's supervisor, Diane. She stated that due to our inquiries, the state was going to take the case before a judge in an attempt to change the children's foster care status from "voluntary" to "involuntary." Diane told Lucas that Endora lied on the agreement she entered into with the State of Alabama.

Our main concern was that if the status was "voluntary," then as soon as Endora got out of jail she could show up and demand to have her kids back. Without her having a job or a place to live, the foster parents would have to surrender them. Now, according to Diane, if Endora showed up tomorrow she would not get the kids back until the case went before a judge. Lucas asked Diane what the chances were, if the status was changed to involuntary, that the state of Alabama would work quickly and efficiently with the state of Missouri so that kids could be placed with us. She responded, not very well. Lucas then asked if they would contact us with the hearing date, as we would like to attend. He was told that they would.

On June 9th, we still hadn't heard from Diane regarding a hearing date. Lucas was unable to sleep the previous night. Something was tugging at his heart. So that morning he placed a follow-up call to Dixie at DHR. Dixie began the conversation by saying "the hearing took place yesterday. I'm surprised that your brother hasn't called you."

"Why would my brother call me?"

"Well, he was in attendance. The judge ordered that you and Rene be contacted."

Lucas asked, "Why wasn't I notified by Diane in advance of this hearing? I told her that we would attend and she said that we would be notified."

"I don't know. Your brother indicated to the judge that he would like custody of the children," Dixie replied.

"My brother? Who hasn't seen the kids for two years, doesn't support them in any way, conspires with their mother to have them placed in foster care with strangers, doesn't tell you that we exist, and now, twenty-four hours after the hearing, still hasn't contacted me?" Dixie didn't know what to say.

Lucas then asked Dixie if it would be possible for us to come visit the children and meet her. She immediately agreed.

About a week later, Lucas and I flew to Alabama and rented a car to drive from Birmingham to Anniston, where the foster family and DHR were located. Neal and Maria, who were vacationing in Tennessee, rented a car and met us there. Dixie picked the kids up from their foster home and met us at the DHR office. The kids had been told that they would see us but were reluctant to come over and hug us when we arrived. Their mother had spent the past two years telling them not to even speak of us, and now here we were. To display any excitement would be a betrayal of Endora.

We all gathered in a playroom inside the DHR building. Fancy Free was very guarded in her reaction to us. Joel became abusive with the toys, banging and throwing them around the room. Their caution in speaking to us lasted only about twenty minutes, until Lucas pulled out pictures he had brought along from their past. That opened both of them up. Children who have been in the situation they have will cling to anything from their pasts. Every time Joel and Fancy Free were scurried off in the middle of the night, they had to leave everything behind. If you asked them they would tell you that their bikes are in storage somewhere and their toys are in storage somewhere else. They really believed that someday they would get their things back.

At one point Dixie asked the four adults to step into a separate room so that she could discuss some things with us. First she wanted to know what we would think of Richie having custody of the children. In disbelief that it would even be considered, we all began to list our reasons: He had given up all parental rights in two divorce agreements, one involving these children. He had abandoned both of his families. As soon as Endora was released from jail he would return the children to her, as he had in the past. He lived in a one-room efficiency apartment, couldn't afford child support, much less childcare, and was sixty years old.

After much discussion regarding Richie, Dixie changed course. She now wanted to know if we had any reason to believe that Fancy Free had been sexually abused. Why would she ask that question? She said they had pictures Fancy Free had drawn. Just like ours. We told her there was no doubt in our minds about it. We shared some of the evidence we had, but didn't tell her everything. After her suggestion that Richie be considered as custodian of the children, we weren't about to reveal everything we knew. Who knew how much of it would be repeated to either of the parents? Before we finished our discussion with Dixie, she told us that she would go to the judge on Monday and request that the children be placed with us.

We left the DHR office about two hours later, having told the kids that we would be back and that we were trying to make it so they could live with us instead of in foster care. The four of us stood out in the vacant parking lot and discussed what had just happened. Lucas had come prepared for the worst, since this ordeal had been going on for four years. The fact that neither Dixie nor Diane had informed us of the hearing and we were not contacted immediately after it only reinforced his distrust in the system. Prior to that meeting, Lucas had contacted an attorney in Anniston, a Mr. Samson. Lucas had been told what he would need to bring along in order for this attorney to file a petition to the court for us to try to get custody, not just placement of the children. Even though Dixie had just told us she intended to file a petition for us to get placement on Monday, we all decided we just couldn't trust that the system would do the right thing for the children this time. So we went by Mr. Samson's law office and left everything in his mailbox.

The following Tuesday, Dixie did call us for additional information regarding our status as foster parents in the state of Missouri. I didn't tell her that since we hadn't heard from her on Monday, our petition had already been filed the day before. Later that week we got word that the hearing date was set for July 29.

Chapter Forty-one

The four of us drove to Anniston on July 28. We had a meeting scheduled with Mr. Samson at 1:30 and were to be in court at 3:00 the next day. We had not yet met our attorney in person, so he spent that time getting to know us and getting a better handle on the case.

Our expectations regarding the hearing were low based on our past experiences in the courtroom. But we were pleasantly surprised this time. Finally, we saw a judge who actually cared about the children. We had waited four long years for that.

When we arrived in the courtroom Endora was already there. None of us had expected her, as she was supposed to be serving her jail sentence, although her presence didn't really surprise us either. Later, from her testimony, we learned that she had been released early because she'd gotten a doctor friend to make restitution for all of her bad checks. We took seats on the opposite side of the courtroom from Endora, but couldn't help stealing glances at her. She was now a blonde, and actually had a decent haircut. She had dressed nicely and wore acrylic nails. She sat with several people we didn't know, who we later learned were from a local church. Richie arrived a short time later and, forced to pick a side, took a seat behind us. He had no representation, so we knew he didn't intend to get into this battle.

The judge listened to three hours of testimony late on a Friday afternoon. Since we had petitioned the court, our attorney called Lucas to the stand first. Again, four attorneys were present: Endora's, one each for the children and for DHR, and ours. Lucas was allowed to elaborate on the horrible lives Joel and Fancy Free had endured, and speak of how we would like to change that. Endora's attorney's plan of attack was to make it look as if Lucas and Richie had conspired to kidnap the children two years ago, then we had contacted DFS to make it look like abandonment. Endora's contention was that if none of that had happened, we would never have been foster parents to her children.

When Dixie was called to the stand it became apparent that she and her supervisor, Diane, now wanted custody of the children to remain with them and the children to remain in Alabama in foster care. It was equally obvious that the attorneys representing the children and DHR disagreed. The questions posed by both of them made it apparent that they felt the children belonged with us. Why had Dixie and Diane changed their position? The only reason would have been because we didn't trust them to get the children placed with us and filed our own petition.

Endora was called to take the stand. She then preceded to be caught in one lie after another. She tried to get the judge to believe that she stayed on the run because she feared our power and money. That she wrote all her bad checks to feed her children and that the children had always been in school. That she had always kept a roof over their heads and never lived out of a car. And, finally, that she had found Jesus for the third time. The first two times were when Joel and/or Fancy Free had been taken from her, when she actually became involved in, bible studies, and would sing Christian songs to Fancy Free over the phone. I'm not sure if she really believed or not, but she could never maintain her churchgoing ways when the kids were around.

The judge let most of this slide because it wasn't worth fighting over. What Endora didn't realize was that the judge had a list of the bad checks sitting in front of him, along with two additional charges pending against her. She was to appear in court in Birmingham in August and then in Pickens County in September, both times for possession of a controlled substance. The Birmingham charge was still pending from her arrest in February of 2003. Two years later she still hadn't had to face a judge on this crime? The judge began to ask Endora some questions of his own. He got her to admit on the stand to writing prescriptions for herself and forging another doctor's name on them. We surmised that she had paid for the drugs with bad checks, as most of the bad checks the judge knew of were made out to various drugstores. Then, presumably, she would go to the streets and sell the drugs to have cash.

During Dixie's testimony the subject of sexual abuse had come up. It was related to Endora's assertion that we had engineered DFS's claiming custody two years ago. We were able to close the hearing by introducing into evidence the Missouri Hospital emergency room doctor's order from two years ago ordering a SAMS test for Fancy Free because he also suspected sexual abuse. The same doctor that had hot lined the children to DFS.

So there you have it. Finally a judge heard our story and saw enough evidence to order, "The children remain in the custody of Alabama DHR." He further ordered that DHR must place the children with us, a kinship family, rather than in foster care. In addition, he directed that DHR file for the ICPC (Interstate Child Placement Compact) process to begin and that it should be completed within thirty days. The ICPC was basically an investigation into Lucas and I, required since we didn't live in the state that had jurisdiction. Throughout this process, Lucas and I were investigated, a home study was done on our house, and someone checked on the welfare of the children. Once the process was complete, a caseworker from Missouri would be assigned to check up on the children. The parents would be able to request supervised visitation

Lucas and I hadn't won our custody battle but we did get placement. This wasn't our first choice for a solution but the children wouldn't know the difference.

Chapter Forty-two

Thirty days after the judge issued the ICPC order, no one had called us or sent us a letter regarding the status of the process. We had been caring for Joel and Fancy Free for thirty days and no one had seen any urgent need to check on them. While I would like to believe that is because my husband and I are so trustworthy, it's more likely just another shortcoming of the system. Fortunately, the children were doing great. They had been in school for two weeks. Fancy Free started playing soccer and Joel joined the Cub Scouts. They both wanted to attend a class at church for the children of divorced and separated homes. Fancy Free started asking children to come over to play. Some weekends we met Neal and Maria at the lake to take the kids boating. Other weekends they went to Neal and Maria's so that we could travel to our own daughters' activities and just have some down time. Fancy Free had a cat at Maria's house, and Joel a turtle. They once again got settled into the routine of a normal life, as normal as their lives could be after their tumultuous early years.

The story really doesn't end here, although I think enough of it has been told for the reader to get an idea of how badly the system needs to change. As soon as the ICPC process is done and we know which state will have jurisdiction over the matter, we plan to petition the court to have the parental rights removed. But we believe it's very possible that Endora will be given one more chance to be a mother to her children. If somehow she can manage to stay out of jail, once a caseworker has been assigned and jurisdiction decided, she would have the right to petition the court to have her children back. With her history, she would not get custody immediately, but the court might ask social services to retain custody and keep them placed with us, and Endora would be given a list of requirements to meet. She would probably have to have a job for three to six months, have a suitable place to live with furniture, be in therapy, and stay on her medications. Then if these conditions are met, we believe she will be given another chance. A lot will depend on the felony drug charges pending against her.

The big question here, that won't be answered by Endora fulfilling any of these requirements, is the suspected sexual abuse of Fancy Free. Also, Endora has proven time and again that she can get a job and even keep it for a period of time, as long as she doesn't have the children. But as soon as she gets them, it falls apart. She can't get out of bed for work or for school. Then she is out of money and on the run.

There are no "do-overs" with the lives of children in abusive situations. Joel and Fancy Free have lost the first six and eight years of their short lives, and nothing can recapture that for them. All the money and therapy in the world won't give them back their innocence. There are thousands of children like them in this country. So why is it so important to social services that their mission be to "reunite the family?" Because where else do they go with all of the abused and neglected children? We must find a way to make the number one priority or mission to "protect the child." If protection can be accomplished concurrently with reunification, that would be the best scenario.

Were the parents concerned about the family unit when they decided it was okay not to feed their child, or physically harm their child? Were the parents concerned about the family unit when they decided that child pornography or sexual molestation was a fun idea? The list could go on and on. Life must be very difficult for social services. What can they do with all those children? Are there enough foster homes?

In our case, if the goal had been different from the start, the children would not have had to endure four more years of abusive treatment. If the mission had been to protect the child, then they would have called on us. No other issue, like jurisdiction, should ever take precedence over the welfare of a child. Judges should be mandated by law to hear the evidence that Family Services has collected. Other legal issues should never take priority over the safety of the child.

If we are going to spend millions of tax dollars to "protect children" then let's do that. If the system is not working as efficiently as it should then we need to be trying to make it better. Our story is just one of many.

Addendum

5/25/06 . . . . .We return to Anniston Alabama with the children. We have had the children for ten months. This is the mother's day in court and the judge will hear this case at 1:30. After listening to almost five hours of testimony, the judge begins his fifteen -minute summation to the parents blasting them for their lack of parental behavior in the past. Endora has met all of the requirements set out by DHR ie. Holding a job, submitting to random drug testing (which she hasn't always passed), psychological evaluation, staying on her medications, attending parenting classes, and providing a suitable home. None of these has addressed the issue of sexual abuse or the criminal charges pending against her (one of these drugs charges has been continued since Feb. 2003 and it is now 2006.) None the less, at the end of the judges speech he will state that "what is in the best interest of the children is not what I'm legally bound , by law, to do."

The children were returned to their mother that day. Even though the judge made it clear that he wanted "the aunts and uncles to be able to speak, by phone, and to visit the children," that has not been allowed to happen.